A Glossary of Islam

Dominique Sourdel and
Janine Sourdel-Thomine

Translated by
Caroline Higgitt

EDINBURGH UNIVERSITY PRESS

First published in France by Presses Universitaires de France, 6 avenue Reille, 75014 Paris, in 2002 as Vocabulaire de l'Islam

First published in English in 2007 by Edinburgh University Press
Edinburgh University Press Ltd
22 George Square, Edinburgh

Typeset in Goudy by
Koinonia, Manchester, and
printed and bound in Great Britain by
Antony Rowe Ltd, Chippenham, Wilts

A CIP record for this book is available from the British Library

ISBN 978 0 7486 2138 5 (paperback)

Ouvrage publié avec le concours du Ministère français chargé de la culture – Centre national du livre.

Liberté • Égalité • Fraternité
RÉPUBLIQUE FRANÇAISE

The publishers thank the French Ministry of Culture – National Book Centre – for kindly granting a translation subvention.

Published with the support of the Edinburgh University Scholarly Publishing Initiatives Fund.

Foreword

Edinburgh University Press is indeed fortunate to have secured for this volume the services of France's two most senior and eminent scholars of Islamic studies, each of them with a track record of some sixty years of publication. France has long had a glittering reputation for scholarship on Islam, but nowadays, because of the dominance of English, many important works in French in this field are not read as widely as they deserve to be.

It is no easy task to provide definitions, but this book has been enriched by two minds rather than one. Indeed, the fruitful collaboration of this distinguished husband-and-wife team has resulted in a glossary of unusual scope, depth and both chronological and geographical range.

It is my hope that this book, ably and imaginatively translated by Caroline Higgitt, will become the first port of call for both general readers and students seeking succinct and solid information in this most topical of fields.

Professor Carole Hillenbrand
Series Editor, 'The New Edinburgh Islamic Surveys'

A

‘ABADA – “To adore [God]”. The root of this word is used to form several other religious terms.

See **‘abd**, **‘ābid**, **‘ibādāt** and **‘ubbād**

‘ABBĀS (al-) – Paternal uncle of **Muḥammad**, belonging to the clan of the **Hāshimids** within the **Quraysh** tribe. They were responsible for the **siqāya** for pilgrims at the pre-Islamic **Ka‘ba** in **Mecca**. He did not accompany his nephew on the **Hijra** and did not rally to him until 630 when Muḥammad occupied Mecca. He was nevertheless looked on favourably in Muslim tradition since he was the ancestor of the **‘Abbāsid dynasty of caliphs**.

See **Ibn al-‘Abbās**

‘ABBĀSIDS – Descendants of **al-‘Abbās**, one of **Muḥammad’s** uncles. They took power as **caliphs** in 750, governing the Islamic empire until 945 despite opposition and uprisings. Thanks to their spiritual prestige, they then retained a nominal authority in **Baghdad** until 1260, thereafter surviving as a puppet **dynasty** in Cairo under the **Mamlūks** until 1517.

See **Hāshimites**

‘ABD, pl. **‘UBUD**, **‘IBĀD**, **‘UBADĀ’** – “Servant, **slave**”. Formed from the root **‘abada**, this word often means “servant [of God]”, a phrase applied to **Muḥammad** in the **Qur’ān** and by extension to all believers, particularly in the formula *al-*

'abd al- faqīr, "humble servant [of God]". – It is also found in theophoric Muslim **names**. Following a well-established Semitic tradition, names such as **'Abd Allāh** or **'Abd al-Raḥmān** quickly became popular in Islamic society. The plural form of this meaning of the word, *'ibād*, is used to mean "humans". – Most commonly, the word has the technical meaning of "slave" and can be replaced by **mamlūk** or *khādim*.

ABDĀL – "Those who substitute one another". In Muslim mysticism, these are **apotropaic saints** who succeed one after the other without any alteration in their number or hierarchy.

See **abrār**, **ghawth** and **quṭb**

'ABD ALLĀH – "**Slave** or servant of God". An expression used not only as an element in the titles of the first **caliphs** but also as the simplest and very popular theophoric personal **name**.

See **'Abd al-Raḥmān** and **Allāh**

'ABD AL-RAḤMĀN – "Servant of the Merciful One". A common Muslim name, it is one of the theophoric personal **names** formed from the **attributes** of God, known as the **Beautiful Names of God**.

See **raḥma** and **Raḥmān (al-)**

'ĀBID, pl. **'UBADĀ'**, **'ĀBIDŪN** and **'UBBĀD** – "Believer" and, for the **Ṣūfīs**, "ascetic".

See **asceticism**, **Zayn al-'Ābidīn**

ABLUTIONS – Necessary to obtain **ritual purity** which is required for ritual prayers (**ṣalāt**) and when making the **Pilgrimage**. – A state of minor impurity, occasioned particularly by the satisfying of natural needs, is cleansed by the ritual of *wuḍū'* (lesser ablution) in an annexe of the **mosque**, the **miḍa'**, or at a fountain of running water, the **hawḍ**, in the centre of the courtyard. – Major impurity, resulting mainly from sexual relations, is cleansed by a more extensive ablution (**ghusl**), a practice that led to a proliferation of baths or **ḥammāms** in Muslim towns.

See **tayammum**

ABRĀR – The "Pure". – One of the names given in the **Qur'ān** to the **Elect** on the Day of Judgement (**yawm al-dīn**). – It is used by **mystics** for a category of **apotropaic saints**.

See **abdāl, ghawth and quṭb**

ABROGATION – Arabic **naskh**. Process whereby the binding nature of a verse from the **Qur'ān** is removed. This can occur when a new verse, called **nāsikh** or "abrogating", contradicts a prescription formulated in a verse revealed at an earlier date, known as "abrogated" (**mansūkh**). For example, the obligation to face **Jerusalem** when carrying out the ritual prayer (**ṣalāt**) was abrogated by a later verse laying down that worshippers should face in the direction of **Mecca**.

ABŪ – "father" or "father of". This term, the **kunya**, forms part of male Muslim personal names.

ABŪ BAKR – First of the **Rāshidūn**, the first four **caliphs** of Islam. Elected by the **community**, he ruled from 632 to 634. He was the father-in-law of **Muḥammad** and one of the **Companions** who accompanied him on the Emigration (**Hijra**) to Yathrib, the city that was to become known as **Medina**.

See **'Ā'isha**

ABUSES (court of) – See **dār al-'adl** and **maẓālim**.

ABYSSINIA – Country to which a number of early Muslims emigrated to escape persecution before going to **Medina** after the **Hijra**.

ACCEPTANCE – Legal term used in contracts, particularly those concerned with **selling**.

See **qabūl**

ACCIDENT – Philosophical term.

See **'araḍ**

ACQUISITION (IKTISĀB) – Theological concept.

See **ash'arism** and **free will**

ACTIVE INTELLECT – See **'aql al-fa''āl (al-)**.

ĀD – **Arab** people of the pre-Islamic period to whom the **Prophet Hūd** spoke.

‘ĀDA – “Custom, usage, **customary law**”.

ADAB – **“Rules of conduct”**, taught in the first centuries of Islam through Persian treatises translated into Arabic and adopted in cultivated circles in the **Baghdad** of the **‘Abbāsid caliphs**. – Subsequently incorporated into the rules of Muslim propriety.

See **adīb**

ADAM – Biblical figure and first human being. His **creation** by God followed the creation of the “world” (**‘ālam**). – He was also the first **prophet** and one whose memory is frequently evoked in the area around **Mecca**.

See **angels**, **Hawwā**, **khalīfat Allāh** and **mīthāq**

‘ADHĀB – Divine “punishment” reserved for the **damned** on the Day of Judgement, **yawm al-dīn**. The announcement of this day by the **prophets** appears in many passages of the **Qur’ān**. It is preceded by the “punishment in the **tomb**” (**‘adhāb al-qabr**).

‘ADHĀB al-QABR – “Punishment in the **tomb**” that, according to the Tradition (**ḥadīth**), is undergone immediately after death by those who are not **martyrs**. It is carried out by **angels**.

ADHĀN – “Call” to ritual prayers or **ṣālat** and consisting of several formulae. These are seven in number for **Sunnīs**: 1. “God is most great” (**Allāh akbar**); 2. “There is no god but Allāh”, the first part of the **shahāda**; 3. “**Muḥammad** is His **messenger**”, second part of the **shahāda**; 4. “Come to prayer”; 5. “Come to salvation (*falāḥ*)”; 6. “God is most great”; 7. “There is no god but Allāh”. – The **Shī‘ites** add an eighth formula: “Come to the best of works”. The **adhān** is chanted from the top of **minarets** by the **muezzin** and repeated at the moment when prayers begin, when it is called the **iqāma**.

ADHRUḤ – Place in Transjordan known for the “Judgement of Adhruḥ”. It was the meeting place, in 658, of the two arbiters (**ḥakam**) charged with the task of resolving the differences between **‘Alī** and Mu‘āwiya who both claimed the right to be

caliph ("successor" of **Muḥammad**).
See **Ṣiffīn**

ADĪB, pl. **UDABĀ'** – "Cultivated man" whose erudition may, but not necessarily, imply a mastery of the **religious sciences** of Islam which are studied rather by a "scholar" (**'alīm**, pl. **'ulamā'**).
See **adab**

'ĀDIL, pl. **'UDŪL** – "Fair-minded person, person of integrity" having the qualities necessary for a witness. – Whence the meaning of "official witness to a deed" whose name will appear on a list drawn up by a judge (**qāḍī**) and who can be called upon to sign legal deeds (**'aqd**). – Sometimes incorrectly translated as "notary".

'ADL or 'ADĀLA – Arabic word meaning firstly "fair and equal division", so giving the meaning "justice" handed out by a sovereign or a **qāḍī**. – For the **Mu'tazilites** it refers to "divine justice". These "rationalisers" claimed that humans have **free will** and that therefore God cannot be held responsible for **evil**. – The notion of virtue was introduced by those moralists who were influenced by Aristotelianism. See **'ādil**, **ahl al-'adl** and **dār al-'adl**

ADMINISTRATIVE REGULATION – Modifying a disposition of the law or **Sharī'a**.
See **qānūn**

ADULTERY – Punished by a "legal sentence" (**ḥadd**).
See **zinā'**

AGHA KHĀN – Present-day title of the spiritual leader of the **Ismā'īlī Nizārī Shī'ites** or neo-Ismā'īlīs.

AḤALLA – Verb referring to the action of "coming out of a state of holiness or purity" having completed the **ḥajj** or **'umra** to **Mecca**.
See **holiness (state of)**, **iḥrām** and **muḥrim**

'AHD – "Pact, treaty". Term used in the **Qur'ān** to refer to the agreements temporarily drawn up by **Muḥammad** with unbelievers.

See **hudna**

AḤKĀM – Pl. of **ḥukm** in the sense of "categories" qualifying **human actions (a'māl)**.

AHL al-'ADL wa'l-TAWḤĪD – "Supporters of divine justice and the Oneness of God", meaning the **Mu'tazilites**.

AHL al-BAYT – "People of the House" of **Muḥammad**. – Expression from the **Qur'ān** which, according to the **Sunnīs**, refers to the wives of Muḥammad. For the **Shī'ites** it means Muḥammad's direct descendants, i.e. his daughter **Fāṭima** with her husband **'Alī** and their children **al-Ḥasan** and **al-Ḥusayn**.

See **Āl Muḥammad**, **Shī'ism**, **imām** and **Shī'ite imāms**

AHL al-ḤADĪTH – "People of the **ḥadīth**" or "upholders of the Tradition", meaning the jurists (**faqīh**). They use the **Qur'ān** and the Tradition (ḥadīth) to determine the rules of religious law (**fiqh**).

See **traditionalism**

AHL al-ḤALL wa'l-'AQD – "Men who bind and unbind". Those who come together to arrive at a **consensus** of the **community**.

AHL al-KAHF – "The Men of the Cave". Arabic name for "The Seven Sleepers". This story, Christian in origin, is told in one of the **sūras** of the **Qur'ān**. – The place usually sited near Ephesus in Anatolia where seven young men persecuted by the Romans were said to have slept for two centuries has become one of the sites for "pious visitation" (**ziyāra**), although the story has also been attached to other locations.

AHL al-KISĀ' – "The People of the Cloak". Name given to the group of Muslims who came to meet a delegation of Christians from **Najrān**. The group consisted of **Muḥammad** who sheltered **'Alī**, **Fāṭima** and their two sons **al-Ḥasan** and **al-Ḥusayn** beneath his cloak. Also known by **Shī'ites** as the "People of the House" (**ahl al-bayt**).

See **Āl Muḥammad**

AHL al-KITĀB – The "People of the Book" or "Possessors of

Scripture". This expression from the **Qur'ān** refers particularly to the Christians and the Jews (who, although they altered it, are considered to have been the first to have received the monotheist revelation on which Islam is founded).

See **Banū Isrā'īl**, **dhimmī**, **naṣārā** and **yahūd**

AHL al-MA'RIFA – Name given to **Ṣūfīs**.

See **'ārif** and **ma'rifa**

AHL al-SUNNA or **AHL al-SUNNA wa'l-JAMĀ'A** – The "Upholders of the **Sunna** and the **community**", meaning those who follow the Tradition (**ḥadīth**) and the rules fixed by the community (**jamā'a**) as opposed to the supporters of "rationalising", politico-religious **movements** such as the **Mu'tazilites** or, more generally, "deviationists".

See **orthodoxy** and **Sunna**

AHL al-ṢUFFA – "The People of the Bench" or "of the Portico". The **Companions of Muḥammad** who lived beneath the gateway forming part of the **mosque** at **Medina**. – Thought to have devoted themselves to a life of **piety** and **poverty**.

AḤMADIYYA – **Religious movement** founded in India by Mīrzā Ghulām Aḥmad (1839–1908), a **Ṣūfī** claiming the rank of **mahdī**. – It divided, in 1914, into two branches, one preaching a radical Islam, the other encouraging intellectual liberalism.

AḤRAMA – Verb describing the action of "entering into a state of holiness or purity" in order to carry out the **hajj** or **'umra** to **Mecca**.

See **holiness (state of)**

AḤWĀL – "States or conditions": pl. of **ḥāl**.

AḤZĀB – "Groups, parties or factions": pl. of **ḥizb**.

'Ā'ISHA – Favourite wife of **Muḥammad** and daughter of his first **Companion**, **Abū Bakr**. – In the course of the divisions in the **community**, she aligned herself against **'Alī** at the Battle of the **Camel** in 656. She died in 678. – Known as **umm al-mu'minīn** ("mother of the believers").

'AJAM (al-) – "Non-**Arabs**", usually referring to Persians.

AKHBĀR – "Stories" or "traditions": pl. of **khabar**.

ĀKHIRA – The "life to come".

See **dunyā**

AKHĪS – Turkish name, perhaps influenced by the Arabic **akhū**, given to members or leaders of medieval associations dedicated to the ideas of the **futuwwa** and who played a politico-religious role in Anatolia in the fourteenth and fifteenth centuries.

AKHLĀQ – Arabic term meaning "morals, ethics" found in the titles of works discussing *tahdhīb al-akhlāq* (the "formation of character") written around the eleventh century. They draw on exhortations to **piety** taken from the **Qur'ān**, Persian manuals on behaviour (**adab**) and traditions from the philosophers of Antiquity who influenced the **falāsifa**. The latter exhort the rational soul (**nafs**), to conquer concupiscent and bestial impulses in order to attain **justice** (**'adl**). – Reflections of this kind supplemented the recommendations and prescriptions of the religious law (**Sharī'a**) which advocate **solidarity** within the **community** and which also define the ethical **economics** of Islam. – The contribution of **Ṣūfism** was to stress trust in God, **tawakkul**, preaching also the idea of personal effort, the indispensable basis of the social virtues required of the good Muslim.

AKHŪ, pl. **IKHWĀN** – "Brother".

See **akhīs**, **Ikhwān** (**al-**), **Ikhwān al-muslimūn** (**al-**) and **Ikhwān al ṣafā'**

'ALAM, pl. **A'LĀM** – "Sign" used, for example, of the marker of the **mawqif** and particularly to mean "standards", "flags" frequently used for religious ceremonies.

'ĀLAM, pl. **'ĀLAMŪN** – "World" in the philosophical and theological sense, meaning the universe, the "contingency" (**ḥadath al-'ālam**) of which is guaranteed by divine **creation**. The word appears in the plural in the **Qur'ān** in the expression **rabb al-'ālamīn** ("master or lord of the worlds"), referring to God.

See **Ash'arism** and **falāsifa**

'ALAWITES – See **Nuṣayrīs**.

'ALAWIYYA or 'ALAWIDS – Dynasty of Hāshimite sharīfs reigning in Morocco since 1635 when it succeeded the Sa'dī dynasty (**Shurafā'**).

'ALAYHI AL-SALĀM – "Peace be on him". – Formula constructed around the word **salām** that must follow the name of any prophet whether spoken or written. A longer formula of blessing, beginning **ṣallā Allāh 'alayhi**, is used for **Muḥammad**.

ALEVIS – Members of **religious movements** revering the memory of **'Alī**. – Today they are found in Turkey, some in Anatolia and others, connected with the 'Alawites or **Nuṣayrīs** of Syria, in the area around the town of Iskandarūn/Alexandretta.

ALEXANDER – See **Dhu' l-Qarnayn**.

'ALIDS – Descendants of **'Alī ibn Abī Ṭālib** amongst whom are the **Imāms** of **Shī'ism**.

See **Hāshimites**, **sayyid** and **sharīf**

'ALĪ al-AṢGHAR – See **'Alī Zayn al-'Ābidīn**.

'ALĪ al-HĀDĪ – Tenth **Imām** of the **Twelver Imāmites** who died in 868 in **Samarra** where the **Shī'ites** venerate his tomb in the mausoleum of the **'Askariyayn** which also houses the tomb of the Eleventh Imām, his son **al-Ḥasan al-'Askarī**.

'ALI al-RIḌĀ – Eighth **Imām** of the **Twelver Imāmīs** who died in 818 in Iran near Ṭūṣ where his tomb, venerated by the **Shī'ites**, has given rise to a sanctuary and the present-day town of **Mashhad**.

ALIF – First letter of the Arabic alphabet seen by mystics as a symbol of the Oneness (**tawḥīd**) of God.

ALIGARH (**Movement**) – Twentieth-century current of thought named after the town in India where the Anglo-Oriental College was established in 1875. The head of the college was Sayyid Aḥmad Khān who led it in the direction of moderate **modernism**.

See **Deoband** (**Movement**)

'ALĪ ibn ABĪ ṬĀLIB – Cousin and son-in-law of **Muḥammad**

whose daughter **Fāṭima** he married; he was removed from power by the **Companions**. – In the struggle against Mu‘āwiya who had seized power under the pretext that he was the cousin of the fourth **caliph ‘Uthmān** and a **Qurashī** of the **Umayyad** clan, ‘Alī was assassinated at **Kūfā** in 661. – His memory is revered by the **Shī‘ites** and the **Twelver Imāmīs** consider him to be their first **Imām**.

See **Adhruḥ**, **‘Alids**, **Najaf** and **Ṣiffīn**

‘ALĪM (al-) – The “Most Wise”. One of the **Beautiful Names of God**.

‘ĀLIM, pl. **‘ULAMĀ’** – “Scholar” in religious matters.

ĀL ‘IMRĀN – “The family of ‘Imrān”. – This expression from the **Qur’ān** means the “family of **Mūsa** (Moses) and of **Hārūn** (Aaron)”, the name ‘Imrān corresponding to that of the biblical Amran, father of Moses and Aaron. – However, in another passage in the Qur’ān, ‘Imrān is referred to as the father of **Maryam** (Mary), in other words, the Joachim of the Apocryphal Gospels.

‘ALĪ ZAYN al-‘ĀBIDĪN – Or ‘Alī al-Aṣghar. The son of **al-Ḥusayn**, third **Shī‘ite Imām** of the **Sevener Ismā‘īlīs** and fourth of the **Twelver Imāmīs**. Famous for his **piety**, he died in **Medina** in 715 where he was buried near the tomb of his uncle the Imām **al-Ḥasan**.

ALLĀH – The **One** God, **Creator** of the universe (**‘ālam**), given, in the **Qur’ān**, attributes such as “powerful”, “wise”, “merciful”, etc. known as the **Beautiful Names of God** in which the theologians have generally seen the expression of eternal attributes distinct from the Divine entity. He revealed the book called the **Qur’ān** to **Muḥammad**.

See **lāhūt**, **ḥamdu li-llāh (al-)** and **mulk li-llāh (al-)**

ALLĀH AKBAR – “God is great”. – **Doxology** repeated (*kabbara* in Arabic) by Muslims in many circumstances of daily life and reproduced in innumerable **inscriptions**. It also forms part of religious ritual, particularly in the **adhān** (call to prayer), during the **ḥajj** and before battle.

ALLĀH A'LAM – "God knows best". – **Doxology** in current usage in daily Muslim life.

ALLĀT – Pre-Islamic divinity mentioned in the **Qur'ān** with al-'Uzza and Manāt.

ALLEGIANCE (oath of) – See **bay'a**.

ALLEGORY – Image invested with a hidden meaning (**bāṭin**) in **Qur'ānic exegesis**.
See **ta'wīl**

ALL-POWERFUL (the) – One of the names given to God.
See **Qadīr (al-)**

ALL-SEEING (the) – One of the names given to God.
See **Baṣīr (al-)**

ALMOHADS – Arabic **al-muwaḥḥidūn**, "upholders of the Oneness of God or **tawḥīd**" – A **religious movement** that gave its name to the Berber **dynasty** that held power in **North Africa** and Muslim Spain from 1130 to 1269. – The founder of the movement, the reformer Ibn Tūmart, settled in the High Atlas Mountains from 1125 preaching a **rigorist** doctrine in the name of a saviour (**Mahdī**), who was in fact himself.

ALMORAVIDS – Arabic **al-murābiṭūn**, "the people of the **ribāṭ**". – Name of the Berber dynasty that ruled in North Africa from 1056 to 1147 and which had its origins in the reformers and warriors of the **jihād** against the inhabitants of the western Sahara. – Capturing Sijilmassa in 1053 and then the area around Ṣuṣ, they established the city of Marrakesh before moving victoriously into Muslim Spain, extending their empire there and in North Africa.

ALMS – There are two kinds of alms: – the term **zakāt** describes almsgiving that is a religious obligation; – the term **ṣadaqa** refers to alms given voluntarily.

ĀL MUḤAMMAD – "The family of **Muḥammad**" in the broad sense of **Hāshimites**. – It was as members of this "family" and as descendants of **al-'Abbās** that the **'Abbāsids** took power in 749. They opposed the **'Alids**, who were also

Hāshimites and who were seen by the **Shī'ites** as the direct descendants of Muḥammad through his daughter **Fāṭima**, the "People of the House" (**ahl al-bayt**) and the "People of the Cloak (**ahl al-kisā'**).

'AMAL – "Legal practice". – Also has the meaning of "**human action**, work" as in the plural **a'māl**.

A'MĀL – "**Human actions**", the object of "categories" of qualification (**ḥukm**) in legal language. – For most Muslim theologians these have a secondary role: only faithfulness to Islam can assure salvation, even if a number of **eschatological** passages in the **Qur'ān** referring to the Day of Judgement (**yawm al-dīn**), stress the importance of good actions. – By contrast, the **rigorist** politico-religious **movement** of the **Khārijites** attaches as much importance to good works as to faith.

See **wazn al-a'māl**

AMĀN – "Safety, protection" – Referring to the guarantee of protection in the "territory of Islam" (**Dār al-Islām**) that a person in authority can give either to a rebel who has surrendered or to a non-Muslim foreigner wishing to travel or live in **Muslim lands**. – It was through the application of this principle that, from the twelfth century, both western and eastern Muslim states were able to draw up commercial treaties facilitating trade with Christian states.

See **musta'min**

AMANA – "To have faith" and "to believe". Several words in religious vocabulary are derived from the root of this word.

See **amān**, **amāna**, **amīn**, **imān** and **mu'min**

AMĀNA – "Sacred trust" that the **Qur'ān** says should be respected. – Interpreted by some authors as meaning the duty of **solidarity** within the Muslim **community**.

AMARA – "To order, to command". This word is the root for several other terms in religious vocabulary. See **amr**, **amīr** and **imāra**.

AMĪN – "Worthy of trust". Honorific added to the name of an **'Abbāsid caliph**. Also applied to various figures in authority in Muslim society including the assistant to the **muḥtasib** also known as *'arīf.*

See **trade associations**

AMĪR – See **emir**.

AMĪR al-ḤAJJ – "Leader of the **ḥajj** caravan" appointed in the Middle Ages by the **caliph** whose representative he was. He took banners and gifts to the **Ka'ba**, a custom that continued into the Ottoman period.

AMĪR al-MU'MINĪN – "Commander of the Faithful", the title given to the **caliph**.

See **mu'min** and **umm al-mu'minīn**

AMĪR al-MUSLIMĪN – "Leader of the Muslims". Title formed by analogy with that of "Commander of the Faithful" and adopted by the **Almoravid** rulers of North Africa who, while not recognising his authority over their empire did not want to sever relations with the **'Abbāsid caliph** in **Baghdad**.

AMĪR al-UMARĀ' – "Supreme Commander" (literally "emir of emirs"). – Title given to the military leader defending the **'Abbāsid caliphs** in the tenth and eleventh centuries.

AMPUTATION – The punishment for theft (**sāriqa**) according to a legal sentence (**ḥadd**). – Still imposed in those Muslim countries where Islamic law (**Sharī'a**) is enforced.

AMR – "Order, commandment". A term that often appears in the **Qur'ān** and which is interpreted in various ways by theologians. – Refers particularly to "God's command" which **was at the origins of** creation and which, according to the **Ash'arites**, explains the evolution of the world without **causality**. – Also refers to "the commandment" given to humankind in **the name of the divine order** by the **ulu'l-amr** or "holders of power".

AMR bi'l-MA'RŪF wa'l-NAHY 'an al-MUNKAR (al-) – "The ordering of the **good** (which is "commended") and the prohibition of the bad (which is "reprehensible")". Formula forming one of the fundamentals of **economic** and social morality in Islam and which gave rise to the office of **ḥisba**

performed by a **muḥtasib**. – A principle of general application, it was adopted by the **Mu'tazilites** for a specific purpose, to justify the intervention of the leader of the **community** in matters of doctrine: thus the Mu'tazilite **caliph** al-Ma'mūn was in a position to force the **'ulamā'** during the **miḥna** to agree that the **Qur'ān** was **created**.

AMULETS – See **magic**.

ANATHEMA (oath of) – See **li'ān**.

ANCESTORS or **ANCIENTS** – See **salaf**.

ANGELS – Arabic *malā'ika*. Spiritual beings mentioned several times in the **Qur'ān**. Servants of God, they were ordered to prostrate themselves before **Adam**, a command that **Iblīs**, also called **al-Shayṭān** (Satan), refused to carry out. – They include **Jibrīl** (Gabriel), the messenger sent to **Muḥammad**, Mikhā'īl (Michael), who bears the **Throne**, Iz-ā'īl, the angel of **death**, and **Israfīl**, the announcer of the Day of Judgement (**yawm al-dīn**). The two angels Munkar and Nakīr carry out the "punishment of the tomb" (**'adhāb al-qabr**).

ANICONISM – Characteristic feature of the cultural and social practices of Islam. It influenced Islamic art, leading to the use of abstract, geometric or floral motifs and the frequent inclusion of **Arabic script**. – While the **Qur'ān** does not proscribe the creation of the "image" or "form" (Arabic *ṣūra*) of living beings, it is forbidden by the Tradition (**ḥadīth**). – Nevertheless, representations of humans and animals appear in secular works of various periods or regions in the Muslim world.

ANIMALS – See **dietary laws**.

ANNIHILATION of SELF – Idea connected with **Ṣūfism**. See **baqā'**, **fanā'** and **ḥaqq**.

ANṢĀR – "Helpers". Name given to the inhabitants of Yathrib, the future **Medina**, who rallied to **Muḥammad** after the **Hijra** to form a single **community** with the **Muhājirūn** (Emigrants).

ANTHROPOMORPHISM – See **tashbīh**.

ANTI-CALIPH – Name applied particularly to Ibn al-Zubayr who, in 683, rebelled in **Medina** against Yazīd, the second **Umayyad caliph**.

ANTICHRIST – See **Dajjāl (al-)**.

APOSTASY – In accordance with a verse in the **Qur'ān** expanded on by a **ḥadīth**, a Muslim who denies his religion is punished by **death**.

See **ḥadd** and **ridda**

'AQABA (al-) – Site between **Minā** and **Mecca** of the secret negotiations in 621 and 622 between **Muḥammad** and the people of Yathrib who were to receive him after the **hijra** and become known as the **anṣār**.

'AQD – "Legal act or deed" applied to a contract or a unilateral declaration (**iqrār**). – Contracts must be drawn up according to precise rules including the establishment of a proposition (**ījāb**) followed by an acceptance (**qabūl**).

'AQĪDA, pl. **'AQĀ'ID** – "Creed, article of faith", consisting of a text several lines long or even a small book with this title. – Should be distinguished from the short "proclamation of faith", the **shahāda**.

'AQĪQA – Sacrifice to be carried out seven days after the birth of a child at the time when he or she receives a name (**ism**).

'AQL – Term with several different definitions: – "reflection", a meaning attested in the **Qur'ān**; – "way to knowledge" as opposed to "knowledge through transmission" (**naql**), and used by the theologians (**mutakallimūn**) and hence "reasoning"; – "intellect" as found in the Greek philosophers and the **falāsifa** (Muslim philosophers) who generally refer to an "active intellect", *al-'aql al-fa''āl*, that is distinct from God and which permits all human intellects to be enriched by an "acquired intellect"; – "intellect" in the doctrines of a number of politico-religious **movements** derived from **Shī'ism**.

See **nafs** and **rūḥ**

'AQL al-FA''ĀL (al) – "Active intellect".

See **'aql**

‘AQLĪ – “Based on reason”.

See **‘ulūm al-‘aqliyya (al-)**

AQṢĀ (al-) – See **masjid al-Aqṣā (al-)**.

ARABIC (language) – (*lugha*). The language of the **Qur’ān**, it has retained the role of liturgical language and is the language of the religious law (**Sharī‘a**).

ARABIC (script) – (*khaṭṭ*). Plays an important role in the life of both Arab and non-Arab Muslims. **Verses** from the Book, the **Qur’ān**, preserved in Arabic script for centuries, have marked the visual appearance of all aspects of the social environment, occurring not only on religious monuments but also in the applied arts and on household objects.

ARABS – Inhabitants of the Arabian peninsula of which **Muḥammad** was one and to whom the **Qur’ān** was revealed, in their own language. – The Arabic-speaking peoples in general, whose Arabisation over the centuries followed their Islamisation. In the surrounding areas, depending on the region, there survive varying numbers of non-Arabised people referred to in the Middle Ages as **‘ajam**. These people now make up the largest proportion of Muslims (particularly the populations in the Indian sub-continent and in South-East Asia). – On the other hand, there are still many non-Muslims among the Arabs, particularly Christians, who preserve an Arab way of life that is independent of Islam.

ARAB TRIBES – Known for their struggles with rival tribes and strong **solidarity** within their own tribe. **Muḥammad** sought to replace these characteristics with a **community** that would unite all Muslims, establishing this new organisation with the “Convention of **Medina**” (**ṣaḥīfa**). – The primacy of the **Quraysh** tribe continued, however, with the **caliph** being chosen from their number.

‘ARAḌ – “accident”, in the philosophical sense.

See **atomism** and **jawhar**

A‘RĀF – Region of the “high places”, mentioned in the **Qur’ān** and which represents an intermediate location between **Paradise** and **Hell**.

‘ARAFĀT – Steep-sided plain not far from **Mecca** and notable for the **Jabal al-Raḥma** (Mountain of Mercy), also known as Mount ‘Arafāt. Pilgrims performing the **ḥajj** visit it to perform the ritual of the "standing" (**wuqūf**) on the ninth day of **dhu’l-ḥijja**.

‘ĀRIF, pl. **‘ĀRIFŪN** – "Knowing". Word used in mystical circles for the "initiated" and more specifically of **Ṣūfīs** who have acquired "knowledge" of the spiritual world (**ma‘rifa**) and who are also called *ahl al-ma‘rifa* ("those endowed with knowledge").

ARITHMETIC – Arabic *‘ilm al-‘adad* or *‘ilm al-ḥisāb*, meaning "science of calculation". Developed in Muslim society to resolve questions arising from the requirements of religious law (**Sharī‘a**) such as problems of **astronomy** related to the orientation of ritual **prayers** or the calculation of the legally determined division of an **inheritance**.

See **jabr**

ARKĀN al-DĪN – "Pillars of the religion". These pillars are traditionally five in number: 1. the profession of faith (**shahāda**), 2. ritual prayers (**ṣalāt**), 3. fasting (**ṣawm**), 4. obligatory alms (**zakāt**), 5. pilgrimage (**ḥajj**). To these individual obligations should be added the collective duty of holy war (**jihād**).

ARMY – See **jund**.

‘ARSH – "Throne" of God. The word appears in the **Qur’ānic** expression *‘ala’l-‘arsh istawā* which is normally understood to mean "He was firm in power", although the formula is taken more literally by **traditionalists**.

See **kursī** and **literalism**

‘AṢABA – "Relations through the male line", who take precedence according to the rules of **inheritance** laid down by religious law (**Sharī‘a**).

See **dhawu’ l-arḥām** and **farḍ**

ASBĀB al-NUZŪL – "Circumstances of the **Revelation**" that can explain the meaning of certain verses in the **Qur’ān**.

ASCENSION OF MUḤAMMAD – See **mi‘rāj**.

ASCETIC – See **ābid**, **‘ubbād** and **zāhid**.

ASCETICISM – Arabic *zuhd.* Inspired by certain recommendations in the **Qur’ān** and dating back to early times, it seems to have opened the way to mystical practices. – It was recommended and generally adopted by the **Ṣūfīs** from the beginning of their movement. – It was particularly favoured by the **brotherhoods** in India who often adopted eccentric practices.

AṢḤĀB al-JANNA – “Companions of the Garden” of **Paradise** mentioned in the **Qur’ān**, i.e. the Chosen.
See **yawm al-dīn**

AṢḤĀB al-MASH’AMA – “Companions of the Left” mentioned in the **Qur’ān** and referring to the **Damned**.
See **yawm al-dīn**

AṢḤĀB al-MAYMANA – “Companions of the Right” mentioned in the **Qur’ān** and referring to the **Elect**.
See **yawm al-dīn**

AṢḤĀB al-NĀR – “Guests of the Fire” of **Hell** mentioned in the **Qur’ān** and referring to the **Damned**.
See **yawm al-dīn**

ASH‘ARISM – **School of theology**, the foundation of which is attributed to al-Ash‘arī (died 935). It adopted a middle way between **traditionalism** and **Mu‘tazilism**, affirming the existence of the divine **attributes** while declaring that these could not be explained, and believing in **free will** understood as an “acquisition” (**kasb** or **iktisāb**). Stressing the power of **irāda** (divine will), it adopted a concept of a universe founded on continuous creation. – It became the most widely spread school of theology in the Muslim world until the modern period.

ASHRĀF – See **sharīf**.

‘ĀSHŪRĀ’ – Religious **festival** that falls on the tenth day of the month of **Muḥarram** when **Shī‘ites** commemorate the violent death of **al-Ḥusayn**, **Muḥammad**’s grandson, at **Karbalā’** in 680. – Celebrated in **Baghdad** from 962 until the arrival of the Sunnī Seljuqs in 1055, it was also celebrated in **Cairo** under the **Fāṭimids** and again in Iran at the time when the **Twelver Imāmīs** became dominant. – In Sunnī areas, the festival involves an additional period of fasting combined, in North Africa, with agrarian rites.

'ASKARIYAYN (al-) – Sanctuary in **Samarra** dedicated to three **Shī'ite imāms** and venerated by the **Twelver Imāmīs**.

See **'Alī al-Hādī**, **āl-Ḥasan al-'Askarī** and **Muḥammad al-Muntazar**

AṢL – "Root", "base": pl. **uṣūl**.

ASLAMA – "To submit to God". Form of the verb **salima**.

See **Islām** and **Muslim**

ASMĀ' al-HUSNĀ (al-) – See **Beautiful Names of God (The)**.

'AṢR (Prayer of al-) – "Afternoon prayer". The third of the five obligatory daily ritual prayers, performed in the mid-afternoon.

See **ṣalāt**

ASSASSINS – Derogatory name given to the members of the **Nizārī Shī'ite Ismā'īlī movement** in Iran and Syria that was characterised by its use of political assassination. The word derives from the Arabic *hashīshī,* "smoker of hashish", although there is no indication that the Nizārīs (also called Bāṭinīs) used hashish before carrying out their attacks. The name "Assassin" was brought back to Europe by the Franks in the crusading period.

ASSOCIATIONISM – Arabic *shirk*. "To associate other gods with God", a concept that is contrary to the doctrine of the oneness of God (**tawḥīd**). For Muslims this is the worst **sin**, one for which Christians in particular are condemned.

See **ithm**, **kāfir** and **mushrik**

ASTRONOMY and **ASTROLOGY** – The "science of the stars" or *'ilm al-nujūm*, the development of which was made possible by advances in **arithmetic**. – Astronomy was useful above all for the calculation of the **qibla** when building a **mosque**. It was also used to fix the end of each month of the Islamic hijri lunar calendar, although custom required that the official method of doing this was by the physical sighting of the **crescent** of the new **moon**. – Astrology was used chiefly for determining a favourable time for certain actions such as a suitable day for founding a new town, as is recorded in the cases of **Baghdad** and **Cairo**.

‘ATĪQ – See **freed slave**.

ATOMISM – Explanation of the universe as being formed of divisible atoms adopted by **Ash‘arite** theologians who reject **causality**, maintaining that all events are dependent on the will of God (**irāda**).

See **jawhar al-farḍ (al-)**

AUDITION (Certificate of) – Awarded to a student. See **samā‘**

AUTHORITY – See **amr**, **caliph**, **Shī‘ism**, **Sunnīs** and **ulu’l-amr**.

AWLIYĀ’ – Plural of *walī* in the **Qur’ānic** sense of “friend, neighbour”, giving also **walī Allāh** (literally “friend of God”) with the sense of “**saint**”. – Also used of the supporters of the **Fāṭimid** regime in Egypt.

See **walāya**

ĀYĀT, sing. **ĀYA** – Proofs of the power of God or “signs of God” which include the **sun** and the **moon**. – Can also mean “verses” of the **Qur’ān**. Each **sūra** contains a variable number of verses, often differing from one another in style and subject.

AYATALLĀH – Or **āyat Allāh**, “sign of God”. – Title given in the twentieth century by the **Shī‘ite Twelver Imāmis** to the supreme interpreter (**mujtahid**), the visible representative of the hidden **imām**.

AYYŪB – Job. Biblical figure referred to several times in the **Qur’ān** as a **prophet**.

AZHAR (al-) – The “shining”. Name given to the Great Mosque (**jāmi‘**) in **Cairo** built by the **Fāṭimids**. The **shaykh** of this mosque is today one of the most important religious and scholarly authorities in the Sunnī world.

'AZĪZ (-al) – "The Powerful". One of the **Beautiful Names of God**.

AZRAQĪS – One of the branches of **Khārijism** whose supporters believed that all those who did not share their ideas should be "physically eliminated", (**isti'rāḍ**) in Arabic. Established in Iraq, they were eliminated in their turn by the **Umayyad** rulers at the end of the seventh century.

See **'Ibāḍites**, **Najadāt** and **Ṣufrites**

B

BĀB – "Door" or "gate" of a building. – In the figurative sense, in **Shī'ite** circles, it was used as a title which varied in meaning according to the **religious movement** adopting it. – Among those given this title, for example, were the interpreters, later given the name of **mujtahid**, of the Twelve **Imāms** of the **Imāmīs**. – The person appointed by the **Ismā'īlī Fāṭimids** to direct the teaching given to the initiates, also known as **dā'ī al-du'āt**, bore the title of *Bāb*. – It was also used by the founder of the **Nusayrīs** and again, in nineteenth-century Iran, by the founder of **Bābism**.

BĀBISM – Politico-religious **movement**, of **Shī'ite** origin, founded in the nineteenth century in Iran by Sayyid 'Alī Muḥammad in opposition to the Shī'ite **'ulamā'** who were seen as corrupt.

See **Bahā'ism**

BADĀ' – "Versatility, inconstancy". Term applied to God by some **Shī'ites** when they seek to justify inconsistencies in their doctrine.

BADR (Battle of) – Battle in which the Muslims of **Medina** led by **Muḥammad** were victorious in March 624 after they ambushed a rich caravan defended by a number of armed **Meccans**. – The victory was supposedly gained as a result of divine intervention mentioned specifically in the

Qur'ān: "For truly God assisted you at Badr when you were helpless".

See **maghāzī**

BAGHDAD – City in Iraq established as the capital in 762 by the **Abbasid caliph al-Manṣūr**. For three centuries it was the politico-religious centre of the Muslim world and acquired a legendary image linked to that of the Golden Age of the Islamic Empire.

See **al-Kāẓimayn** and **Madīnat al-salām**

BAHĀ'ISM – Politico-religious **movement** derived from **Shī'ism**, founded in Iran in the nineteenth century by a former Bāb named Bahā' Allāh ("Splendour of God"). – His followers launched several attacks on the ruling powers and were accused of heterodoxy, whilst surviving, often more or less underground, in Iran, India and a number of other countries.

BAKTĀSHIYYA – **Ṣūfī brotherhood**, taking its name from its founder Ḥājjī Bektash (died 1270) that became popular particularly in the Ottoman Empire.

BALANCE or **SCALES** – See **mīzān**.

BANŪ – Pl. of the word **ibn** ("son"). Used to indicate members of a clan or **tribe** and, more generally, the "descendants" of a known ancestor, whence members of a **dynasty**.

BANŪ 'ALĪ, HĀSHIM, etc. – See **'Alids**, **Hāshimites**, etc.

BANŪ ISRĀ'ĪL – "Sons of Israel". Expression used in the **Qur'ān** to indicate both the Jews of **Medina** and the Jews in general.

See **ahl al-kitāb**, **dhimmī**, **Khaybar**, **monotheism**, **taḥrīf** and **Yahūd**

BAQĀ' – "Existence in God". – State of spiritual ecstasy reached by certain **Ṣūfīs** after annihilation of self (**fanā'**).

BARAKA –"Blessing". Term describing a "beneficent force" of divine origin bringing about happiness and prosperity. – Much used in daily language, particularly in **greetings**, it refers especially to the power of a **saint** to bestow blessings on whom they wish. – This power may also be accessed through certain objects or places popularly believed to be sacred that then become known as **mazārs** (“objects of pious visitations”). – It can also be obtained by the use of amulets and other talismans.

See **magic** and **mutabarrak**

BARZAKH – “Interval”. Term used in the **Qur’ān** with the sense of “intermediate place”, boundary between **Hell** and **Paradise**.

BASHARA – “To rejoice in good news”.

See **bashīr** and **bushrā**

BASHĪR (**al-**) – “The Messenger”. Name given to **Muḥammad**.

See **bushrā**

BASIN – See **ḥawḍ**.

BASIN (**Festival of the**) – **Shī’ite festival**. See **Ghadīr Khumm**.

BAṢĪR (**al-**) – “The All-Seeing”. One of the **Beautiful Names of God**.

BASMALA – The Arabic phrase **bismillāh al-raḥmān al-raḥīm**, “in the name of God the Compassionate, the Merciful”, which appears at the beginning of all but one **sūra** of the **Qur’ān**. – It is recited before all important actions in everyday life and is placed at the beginning of every piece of writing whether a literary work, a proclamation, a legal document or a mere letter.

BATHS – See **ḥammām**.

BĀṬIL – Term meaning “null” in a legal sense or “**vain**” in a moral sense.

See **fāsid**

BĀṬIN – “Hidden meaning” of the **Qur’ān**, the search for which forms the basis of the esoteric **exegesis** pursued by **Shī‘ites** and the followers of **Ṣūfism**.

See **ta’wīl**

BĀṬINIYYA – “Followers of the hidden meaning”. – Name given to the **Ismā‘īlī Shī‘ites** for whom the **Qur’ān** has an exterior meaning (**ẓāhir**), known to all, but also a hidden meaning (**bāṭin**) which justifies the claims of the **'Alid imāms** in particular to possess special qualities of infallibility (**'iṣma**) and therefore to be visited with supreme power.

BATTLES of MUḤAMMAD – Once settled in **Medina**, **Muḥammad** was involved in several "battles" (**maghāzī**) against the **Meccans**. These enabled him to triumph eventually and to return victorious to his native city. The main engagements were those at **Badr**, **Uḥud** and the Battle of the Trench (**Khandaq**). – There was also fighting against other Arabian tribes as at **Ḥunayn** and later further afield with the expedition to **Tabūk**, which already aimed at Syria and paved the way for the "Great **Conquests**".

BAY' – Legal term.

See **selling**

BAY'A – "Oath of allegiance" amongst **Sunnīs** sworn by the **community** of Muslims, often in the person of one of its chief representatives, to the **caliph**, thus conferring on him the legitimacy of his power. – First sworn to **Muḥammad** on the occasion of the **bay'at al-riḍwān**.

See **riḍwān** (or "oath of satisfaction"), also known as **bay'at al-shajara**

See **shajara** ("oath of the tree"), it was used during the **Umayyad** and '**Abbāsid** periods to retain power within the same dynasty. – The oath made by a novice **Ṣūfī** to his master is also called **bay'a**.

BAYRAM –"Festival" in Turkish. See **büyük bayram** and **küçük bayram**.

BAYT al-'ATĪQ (al-) – "The ancient house". Name given to the **Ka'ba**.

BAYT al-ḤARAM (al-) – "The sacred house". Name given to the **Ka'ba**.

BAYT al-ḤIKMA – "House of Wisdom". Name of the academy founded by the '**Abbāsid caliph** al-Ma'mūn in **Baghdad** at the beginning of the ninth century where the texts of the scholars and philosophers of antiquity were translated in **Arabic**.

See **dār al-ḥikma** and **ḥikma**

BAYT al-MAQDIS – "House of sanctity". Medieval name for **Jerusalem**, the ancient name of Aelia being preserved for only a short time in Arabic and later replaced by al-Quds.

BAYYINA – "Proof" in the legal sense. – According to the rules of religious law (**fiqh**), proof can be produced in three different ways: "confession" (**iqrār**), which can give rise to a written deed, "evidence" (**shahāda**) and "judicial oath" (**yamīn**).

See **dalīl** and **ḥujja**

BĀZĀR – Persian word equivalent to the Arabic **sūq** or **souk** and referring to **markets** in the Persian and Turkish areas.

See **trade associations**, **ḥisba** and **qaysariyya**

BEAUTIFUL NAMES OF GOD – Arabic *al-asmā'al-ḥusnā.* Names applied to God in the **Qur'ān** which adds "Pray to Him using these names". – According to the Tradition, they are 99 in number and include the **attributes** of God (**ṣifāt**). – The repetition of this litany has always been practised by the **Ṣūfīs** who make it one of the bases of their mystical seances (**majlis**). It is also recommended that it be repeated with the aid of prayer beads, the **subḥa**.

BEG – See **bey**.

BEGGARS – See **sā'ilūn**.

BEKTASHIS – See **baktāshiyya**.

BELIEF – Held by the believer (**mu'min**).

See **īmān**

BELIEVER, **BELIEVERS** – **Qur'ānic** notion.

See **mu'min**

BENEVOLENT (the) – One of the **Beautiful Names of God**.

See **Laṭīf (al-)**

BEY or **BEG** – Turkish word that generally took the place of the Arabic amīr to describe an **emir** in the conquered regions of the **'Abbāsid** Empire. The term subsequently became very common during the period of the Ottoman Empire.

BID‘A – "Doctrinal innovation". Term used in religious law (**fiqh**) to describe any practice or doctrine contrary to the earliest form of Islam. – Innovation is condemned and it is the duty particularly of the **caliph** to resist it.

BILĀ KAYF – "Without seeking to understand how". – Formula used particularly by **Ash'arite** theologians to defend the doctrine of divine **attributes**.

See **kayf**

BIOGRAPHIES – Rare in Arab-Muslim literature apart from the **Sīra** of **Muḥammad**. There are many biographical dictionaries (**ṭabaqāt**), however, that form an important part of scholarly literature.

BIRR – **Qur'ānic** term.

See **piety**

BIRTH – Marked by different popular customs including that of reciting the formula of the call to prayer (**adhān**) into the baby's right ear. – A sacrifice, the **'aqīqa**, takes place seven days after a birth. – Later, male children undergo the ritual of circumcision (**khitān**).

BISĀṬ – "That which is laid on the ground" in **mosques**.

See **sajjāda** and **carpet**

BISMILLĀH al-RAḤMĀN al-RAḤĪM – sometimes shortened to **bismillāh**, particularly in everyday oral usage.

See **basmala**

BLACK STONE (the) – Arabic *al-hajar al-aswad.* Sometimes also called *al-hajar al-mustalam,* "the stone that is touched". – Stone embedded in the wall of the **Ka'ba**, already the object of veneration before the advent of Islam. The pilgrims touch it when performing the circumambulation (**ṭawāf**) at the time of the **ḥajj** or the **'umra**.

BLESSINGS – See **baraka** and **curse**.

BOHORĀS – Local name of the **Shī'ites** descended from the **Musta'lian Ismā'īlīs** who settled in India.

BOOK, (PEOPLE of the) – See **ahl al-kitāb**, **kitāb** and **muṣḥaf**.

BOOTY – Legal term.

See **ghanīma**

BRIGANDAGE – Arabic *qaṭ' al-ṭarīq*, literally "barring the way" of a traveller. – Crime punished by a legal sanction (**ḥadd**) depending whether the brigand has caused terror (exile), robbed (**amputation**) or both robbed and killed the traveller (**capital punishment**).

BROTHERHOODS – (**ṭarīqa**). **Ṣūfi** groups adopting particular practices leading to **ecstasy**, or "spiritual paths". – They first emerged in the thirteenth century and led to the founding of lodges (**khanqāhs**), known as **tekkes** in the cities of the Ottoman empire.

See **Baktāshiyya**, **Khalwatiyya**, **Kubrawiyya**, **Mawlawiyya**, **Naqshabandiyya**, **Qādiriyya**, **Qalandariyya**, **Rifā'iyya**, **Sanūsiyya**, **Shādhiliyya**, **Suhrawardiyya**, **Chishtiyya** and **Tijāniyya**

BROTHERS – See **akhū** and **ikhwān**.

BROTHERS (the), **MUSLIM BROTHERHOOD**, **SINCERE BROTHERS** – See **ikhwān (al-)**, **ikhwān al-muslimūn (al-)** and **ikhwān al-Ṣafā**.

BURĀQ – Name of the mythical beast that carried **Muḥammad** from **Mecca** to **Jerusalem** and to the Seventh Heaven in the narratives describing the "Night Journey" (**isrā'**) mentioned in the **Qur'ān** and often also called the "Ascension"(**mi'rāj**).

BURDA – **Muḥammad**'s mantle or cloak, one of a number of relics today in **Istanbul** having once formed part of the treasury of the '**Abbāsid caliphs**. – Name of a famous poem in honour of Muḥammad for which the author was rewarded by Muḥammad with the gift of his cloak.

BURHĀN – "Argument or proof" which, in the **Qur'ān**, expresses the strength of God. Derived from this is a second meaning of "miracle".

BURQA' – From the Arabic *burqū'*. – Long, loose-fitting garment designed to cover entirely a woman's body leaving only some holes through which to see. – Its use, inspired by a strict interpretation of various injunctions in the **Qur'ān**, continues, particularly in Afghanistan. See **ḥijāb**, **chador** and **veil**.

BUSHRĀ – "The good news". The **Qur'ān** uses this term to describe the message brought by **Muḥammad**, who is called **bashīr**, "the messenger".

See **hudā**

BÜYÜK BAYRAM – Turkish name for the "Great Festival" of the **Sacrifice** known in Arabic as **al-'īd al-kabīr**.

See **küçük bayram** and **festivals**

C

CAIRO – Arabic *al-Qāhira*, the "Victorious". City in Egypt established as their residence by the **Fāṭimid caliphs** in 969. It remained the capital of **Ismā'īlī Shī'ism** for more than two centuries. – With the return to **Sunnism**, and the establishment of many madrasas, Cairo has remained until the present day one of the principal cultural centres of Islam.

See **Azhar (al-)** and **dār al- ḥikma**

CALENDAR – Based on the movements of the **moon**, it begins from the date of the **hijra**, 16 July 622, and consists of twelve lunar **months** of 29 or 30 days. The year therefore has 355 days, ten fewer therefore than the solar calendar. – Today, with the exception of Saudi Arabia, the lunar calendar is no longer used except for religious dates.

See **crescent moon**

CALIPH – (**khalīfa**). "Successor" of **Muḥammad** and then "Leader of the **community**" known as **amīr al-mu'minīn** ("Commander of the Faithful"). Later the term **imām** was used for the temporal and spiritual master of the Muslim Empire that became fragmented with the advent of the '**Abbāsids**. – In the tenth century, rival caliphates to the caliphate of **Baghdad**, the **Umayyad** caliphate in Cordoba and the **Fāṭimid** caliphate in Cairo, were of relatively short duration. As for the 'Abbāsid state, it lasted until 1260 although, from the tenth century, the caliph retained only his religious prestige, delegating his other functions to **amirs** or **sultans**. – A descendant who took refuge in Cairo after the Mongol invasion made it possible to re-establish a caliphate, but one whose only function was to confer power on the **Mamlūk** sultans who reigned over the areas of Syria and Egypt. Eventually, after conquering Egypt in 1517, the Ottoman sultans suppressed this survival and carried out the functions of caliph themselves without ever officially assuming this title. – In 1924, Mustafa Kemal (Atatürk) abolished the caliphate, giving rise to protests from various movements but no enduring political repercussions. The states that were formed in the twentieth century confined themselves to sovereigns or presidents who held temporal power. In 1925, Shaykh ʻAbd al-Razīq in Cairo wrote a treatise entitled *Islam and the Bases of Power* which established the doctrinal grounds for the separation of spiritual and temporal power. However, this work was not universally accepted.

CALL TO PRAYER – See **adhān**.

CAMEL (**Battle of the**) – Important battle which took place near Basra in Iraq in December 656 after the assassination of the third **caliph ʻUthmān** and which involved the early Muslims, mainly the **Companions of Muḥammad**. The supporters of **ʻAlī**, on one side, were opposed by the supporters of Talha and al-Zubayr supported by **ʻĀʼisha**, Muḥammad's widow, on the other. It ended with the death of Talha and al-Zubayr. The battle takes its name from the presence of a camel bearing the palanquin in which ʻĀʼisha travelled.

CAMI – Turkish name for a Great Mosque (**jāmiʻ**) in Arabic.

CAPITAL PUNISHMENT – Legal death sentence in the case of **apostasy** (**ridda**), an insult (**sabb**) to **Muḥammad**, adultery by a **woman** (**zināʼ**) and, finally, **banditry**.

See **ḥadd**

CARAVANSARAY – See **khān** and **ribāṭ**.

CARMATHIANS – See **Qarmaṭī**.

CARPET or **RUG** – Arabic *bisāṭ*. Essential items in the furnishing of a **mosque**, they cover the floor where the faithful prostrate themselves (**sujūd**).

See **sajjāda**

CATEGORIES of HUMAN ACTIONS – See **ḥukm**.

CAUSALITY – Only the rationalising **Mu'tazilites**, following the philosophers of Antiquity, interpreted the universe as governed by **determinism**.

See **atomism** and **creation**

CAUSE – In the theological sense.

See **sabab**, pl. **asbāb**. In **qiyās**.

See **'illa**

CAVE (Men of the) – Mentioned in the **Qur'ān**.

See **ahl al-kahf**

CHADOR – Garment worn by women, particularly in Iran, entirely covering the body, leaving only the upper half of the face exposed.

See **burqa'**

CHAIN OF TRANSMITTERS – In the **ḥadīth** and **Ṣūfism**.

See **isnād** and **silsila**

CHARITABLE FOUNDATIONS – The most common kind of pious works, usually taking the form of generous private endowment of religious or charitable buildings, or buildings of public utility. – Their establishment and upkeep were ensured by "inalienable property" (**waqfs**) (or *habous* in the West) set up by dignitaries or rich individuals. – The appearance of medieval towns was transformed by the construction of large numbers of such buildings, including **mosques**, **madrasas**, **mausoleums**, **baths** (**ḥammām**), **hospitals** (**maristān**) and **public fountains** (**sabīl**).

CHARITABLE WORKS – See **charitable foundations**, **piety** and **waqf**.

CHISHTIYYA – **Ṣūfī fraternity** deriving its name from the area of Chisht in Afghanistan. – Flourished particularly in India.

CHRISTIANS – See **Naṣārā**.

CIRCUMAMBULATION – Religious practice.

See **ṭawāf**

CIRCUMCISION – Arabic *khitān*. Recommended by tradition although not mentioned in the **Qur'ān**, it is considered to be a typically Muslim practice. Takes place when a boy is about seven years old and is linked to a family festival.

See **propriety**

CIVIL STATUS – Laid down by religious law (**fiqh**). – Discriminates between Muslims who are governed by the rules of religious law (**Sharī'a**), which includes specific dispositions for free men, **women** and **slaves**, and non-Muslims who are assigned to an inferior rank in Muslim society but are allowed to practise their religion within the confines of their community provided that they observe their fiscal obligations and obey the restrictions imposed on them by their status as **dhimmī** (particularly **Jews** and **Christians** who are considered to be People of the Book (**ahl al-kitāb**)).

See **personal names**

CLIENT, **CLIENTS** – See **mawlā** and **mawālī**.

COINAGE – Minted from the later seventh century and decorated with inscriptions in Arabic script. – As well as providing historical information, these consist mainly of religious texts with phrases such as the **shahāda** or verses from the **Qur'ān**.

COLLEGE – See **madrasa**.

COME to the BEST WORK – Supplementary phrase appearing in the **adhān** (call to prayer) of the **Shī'ites**; its use is a sign of their dominance in a particular area.

See **hayya 'alā khayr al-'amal**

COME TO THE PRAYER (**ṣalāt**) – Phrase appearing in the text of the **adhān** (call to prayer) which precedes the prayer.

COMMANDMENT – See **amara**, **amīr** and **amr**.

COMMUNITY – Arabic *umma* and **jamā'a**. The creation in **Medina** of the community of "believers" (**mu'minūn**) was recorded by a document, the **ṣaḥīfa**. – Its members were required to practise **solidarity** and support their leader, **Muḥammad**, a rule which has continued with regard to the "holders of power" (**ulū'l-amr**), despite personal disagreements and rivalries between the different religious movements that have arisen over the centuries. – It was the task of the community to choose the **caliph** through the oath of allegiance (**bay'a**) and to provide the basis for the consensus (**ijmā'**), seen as one of the fundamental principles of religious law (**fiqh**), at least by most jurists (**faqīh**).

COMPANIONS of MUḤAMMAD – Called **ṣaḥāba** and often quoted as transmitters of the traditions (**ḥadīths**) the origins of which they guarantee at the beginning of each "chain" (**isnād**). They are listed in three categories: those that fought at **Badr**, those that fought at **Uḥud** and those that fought in the Battle of the Trench (**Khandaq**).

See **Anṣār**, **Muhājirūn** and **Tābi'ūn**

COMPANIONS of the RIGHT or COMPANIONS of the GARDEN and COMPANIONS of the LEFT or COMPANIONS of the FIRE – **Qur'ānic** expressions contrasting the **Elect** and the **Damned** on the Day of Judgement (**yawm al-dīn**).

See **aṣḥāb al-janna**, **aṣḥāb al-mash'ama**, **aṣḥāb al-maymana** and **aṣḥāb al-nār**

COMPULSION – Legal term.

See **ikrāh** and **jabr**

CONCUBINES – Religious law (**Sharī'a**), which authorises polygamy of no more than four wives, also authorised sexual relations with female slaves (**jāriya**), in the days of **slavery**.

See **women**, **marriage** and **umm al-walad**

CONFESSION –Legal term.

See **bayyina** and **iqrār**

CONQUESTS or GREAT CONQUESTS – Arabic *al-futūḥ*, pl. of *fatḥ*. Expression used by early writers and historians when referring to the military victories of the seventh century following the death of **Muḥammad**, particularly during the reign of the **caliph 'Umar** (634–44). – As a result, Muslims occupied the lands of the Byzantine and Sasanian Empires, calling this territory the "House of Islam" (**Dār al-Islām**). – The administrative problems that arose concerning booty (**ghanīma**), the tax system of **dhimmīs** and the status of the occupied **land** were gradually resolved. The same solutions were then applied at the time of later conquests.

See **jizya**, **kharāj**, **mawlā** and **muwalladūn**

CONSENSUS – Legal term.

See **ijmā'**

CONSTITUTION of MEDINA – See **ṣaḥīfa**.

CONTINGENCY of the WORLD – See **ḥadath al-'ālam**.

CONVERSION, CONVERTS – Conversion to Islam is simple, consisting of the recitation of the **shahāda** in the presence of **witnesses**. Except in exceptional cases, a convert who reverts to his former religion will be accused of **apostasy**, a crime for which the legal punishment (**ḥadd**) is the death penalty.

See **capital punishment**

COURT of LAW – See **dār al-'adl**.

"CREATED" QUR'ĀN – Arabic *makhlūq*. View of the **Mu'tazilites** in opposition to that of the **traditionalists** and the majority of theologians (**mutakallimūn**).

See **divine attributes**, **kalām Allāh** and **lafẓ**

CREATION – Arabic *khalq*. God created the contingent universe (**'ālam**) *ex nihilo* by a "command" (**amr**). The description of creation in the **Qur'ān** is similar to that in Genesis in the Bible. He also created **Adam** and **Eve** (**Ḥawwā'**) who were expelled from the Garden of **Paradise** for their disobedience. Unlike in Christianity, however, this "original sin" had no repercussions for their descendants. – The creation of the world is understood by most Islamic scholars as continuous. It excludes or at least limits human **free will**.

See **Ash'arites**, **dahriyya**, **determinism**, **Mu'tazilites** and **tawallud**

CREATOR (the) – One of the **Beautiful Names of God**.

See **Khalīq (al-)**

CRESCENT MOON – *hilāl*. Observation of the moon is traditionally necessary in order to determine the end of the **months** of the Islamic **calendar** which follows the cycles of the moon, most importantly to announce the beginning and end of the fast of **Ramaḍān**. – It has become a symbol of Islam and today appears on the flags of a number of Muslim countries. It is also used in connection with the humanitarian organisation, the "Red Crescent" (by analogy with the Red Cross).

CURSE – See **la'na, li'ān** and **mubāhala**.

CURSED ONE (the) – See **rajīm (al-)**.

CUSTOM – Arabic *'āda*.

See **customary law**

CUSTOMARY LAW – Arabic *'āda* and *'urf*. Religious law (**fiqh**) accepts the validity of the customs of a particular region provided that they are not contrary to the **Qur'ān** and the **Sunna**, which is to say to the principles of the law (**Sharī'a**).

D

ḌABṬ – In the language of **mysticism**, "the overcoming of passions".

DAHRIYYA – "Materialism". Condemned by the theologians (**mutakallimūn**) as a doctrine that denies the **creation** of the universe, affirming instead that it is **eternal**. – Can also refer to other currents of thought held by deviationists.

See **ilḥād**

DĀ'Ī, pl. **DU'ĀT** – "Propagandist" or "missionary" practising **da'wa**. – Some of these figures played an important role in the taking of power by the **'Abbāsids** or in the functioning of the **Fāṭimid** regime and also, at a later date, in the propagation of the **Ismā'īlī** doctrine and the neo-Ismā'īlī doctrine of the **Nizārīs**.

See **dār al-ḥikma**

DĀ'Ī al-DU'ĀT – "Supreme **Dā'ī**" (lit. "dā'ī of dā'īs"). Head of propaganda at the time of the **Fāṭimids**. Known as the **Bāb**, he was the chief interpreter of the **caliph**.

DĀ‘ĪF – "Weak". In legal language this adjective is used of a tradition (**ḥadīth**) based on too few pieces of evidence.

See **ḥasan**, **mashhūr**, **mutawātir**, **qudsī** and **ṣaḥīh**

DĀ‘Ī MUṬLAQ – "Absolute **Dā‘ī**". Title given, for example, by the **Musta‘lian Ismā‘īlī Shī'ites** known as **Bohras** to their highest authority.

DAJJĀL (al-) – "The Liar" or Antichrist. It is believed that this figure will appear at the end of the world and will be defeated by **‘Īsā**/Jesus or by the **Mahdī**.

DAKKA – Platform or raised area in the prayer hall of a Great Mosque (**jāmi‘**) where people sit to read the **Qur'ān**.

DALĪL, pl. **DALĀ'IL** and **ADILLA'** – "Sign, argument, rational proof". – To give it greater demonstrative force, this word is sometimes accompanied by an adjective coming from the word **‘aql (reason)**, as in the expression *al- dalā'il al-‘aqliyya* ("rational arguments").

ḌAMĀN – "Guarantee" in the language of religious law (**fiqh**). – In the case of a dispute after a **sale**, it is generally required of the seller, as is usually specified in the legal deed (**‘aqd**).

DAMASCUS – Capital of the **Umayyad caliphs**. One of the oldest monumental Great Mosques (**jāmi‘**), the "Umayyad Mosque", was built here.

DAMNED (the) – Humans condemned by God to **Hell** on the Day of Judgement (**yawm al-dīn**). – Term that frequently appears in the oldest verses of the **Qur'ān**.

See **aṣḥāb al-mash'ama** and **aṣḥāb al-nār**

DĀR – "Dwelling, palace, territory".

DĀR al-‘ADL – "House of justice" (**‘adl**) built in **Damascus** by Nūr al-Dīn in the twelfth century for the examination of appeals against military requisitions or the decisions of administrators; the equivalent of the earlier institution of **maẓālim** conducted by the **caliphs**. – A similar institution is found at a slightly later date in **Cairo** in the residence of the

sultan, who was present at hearings.

See **ruq'a**

DĀR al-ḤADĪTH – "House of Tradition". Institution devoted to the teaching of Tradition (**ḥadīth**). – The first of these establishments was established in 1170 in **Damascus** during the reign of Nūr al-Dīn to train traditionists (**muḥaddithūn**).

See **madrasa**

DĀR al-ḤARB – "House of War" as opposed to "House of Islam" (**Dār al-Islām**). – Territory not yet conquered, that Muslims must attempt to conquer by means of "war" *(ḥarb)* with no possibility of peace (**ṣulḥ**). Truces (**hudna**) can nevertheless be declared in principle for a period of ten years. See **jihād**.

DĀR al-ḤIKMA – "House of Wisdom". Institution set up in **Cairo** by the **Fāṭimid caliph** al-Hākim in 1005 to teach **Ismā'īlī** doctrine spread subsequently by missionaries (**dā'ī**).

DĀR al-'ILM – "House of Science", a medieval expression meaning "library".

See **khizāna**

DĀR al-IMĀRA – In the first centuries of Islam, "palace, residence of the **amir**" who governed a "province" (**wilāya**).

DĀR al-ISLĀM – "House of Islam". – Territory conquered by Muslims and subjected to the religious and social laws of the **Sharī'a**.

See **Dār al-Ḥarb** and **Dār al-Ṣulḥ**

DĀR al-ṢULḤ – "House of **ṣulḥ**". Non-Muslim territory that had concluded a treaty with **Muḥammad**. This was temporarily the situation in the cases of the Christian city of **Najrān** and the Jewish oasis of **Khaybar** in Arabia, but not for the regions invaded by the Muslims after the **conquests** following the death of Muḥammad that were obliged to submit to the status of **dhimma**.

See **Dār al-Ḥarb**, **Dār al-Islām** and **Dār al-Ṣulḥ**

ḌARAR – "Damage, prejudice". Term which appears in the wording of every legal deed (**'aqd**), particularly in the case of a **sale** where the rights of one of the parties are protected.

See **damān** and **selling**

DARB al-ḤAJJ – "Road followed by pilgrims going to **Mecca**". These routes were partially created during the Middle Ages to facilitate the crossing of the deserts of Arabia from Basra and **Baghdad** in Iraq, **Damascus** in Syria and **Cairo** in Egypt.

DĀRGĀH – In India the tomb of a saint, usually a venerated **Ṣūfī** who as a **pīr** or **shaykh** had become the leader of a brotherhood.

ḌARŪRA – In the language of religious law (**fiqh**), "necessity", a situation in which an action that is "forbidden" (**ḥarām**) is permitted.

DA'WA – "Politico-religious call, propaganda, mission". In a general sense, call to **conversion** to Islām. – Historically, an indispensable instrument in the development of revolutionary **religious movements** often culminating in the establishment of new **dynasties** or regimes. The Fāṭimid **da'wa** relied on a hierarchical organisation based in **Cairo** which produced a large number of missionaries (**dā'ī**) who were sent out to all areas.

See **Dār al-Ḥikma**

DAWLA – "State, empire, **dynasty**". In certain periods, rulers took names or titles formed from this word, for example Sayf al-Dawla, "sword of the State". Such titles were generally conferred by the **caliph**.

DĀWŪD – David. Biblical figure viewed in the **Qur'ān** as a prophet and a king whom God made **khalīfa** ("successor") to earlier sovereigns "on earth"; whence the use of the word for the successors of **Muḥammad**.

DEATH – Arabic *mawt*. According to the **Qur'ān**, decreed by God and followed by the "punishment of the **tomb**" (**'adhāb al-qabr**), **resurrection** and the Day of Judgement (**yawm al-dīn**). – Linked in various narratives to the action of **angels** among which are Azrā'īl and the **interrogating angels** Munkar and Nakīr. – Involves funeral rites laid down by jurists (**faqīh**) in addition to traditional local customs, such as the washing of the body, wrapping in a shroud, prayer (**ṣalāt**) in a **mosque**, and burial with the face of the dead person turned towards **Mecca** in a grave oriented towards the **qibla**. No monument should be placed over the grave.

See **capital punishment**

DEMONS – See **jinns** and **Iblīs**.

DEOBAND – City in India where an Islamic university was established in the nineteenth century. Its professors preached about the need to return to the fundamentals of early Islam and defended the idea of a rigorist school which opposed the **modernist** theories of the **Aligarh** school.

DERVISH – From the Persian **darwīsh**, "poor man". The equivalent of the Arabic **faqīr**, it was applied particularly to the **Ṣūfī** members of a number of **brotherhoods** in Anatolia and Iran.

DETERMINISM – Arabic **tawallud**. View of the universe based on a chain of causes. Defined by the **Mu'tazilites** in an attempt to rationalise the concept of **creation**.

See **atomism** and **causality**

DEVIATION, DEVIATIONISM – See **heresy** and **ilḥād**.

DEVSHIRME – Institution of the Ottoman Empire. With the power to levy young Christians captured from their families, it continued until the beginning of the eighteenth century. Once **converted** to Islam and trained in their future functions, they became government "**slaves**", sometimes freed slaves, working for the army, particularly as **Janissaries**, or for the administration, where they might rise to the highest positions.

DHABḤ – "Act of slaughtering" animals according to the regulation which allows the consumption of such meat, then regarded as "permitted" (**ḥalāl**). – It is also used for the sacrifice that takes place at **Minā** during the **ḥajj** and at the time of the "Major Festival" (**al-'īd al-kabīr**).

See **dietary laws**

DHABĪḤA – "Victim" to be sacrificed in fulfilment of a vow at **Minā** during the **ḥajj** and at the time of the "Major Festival" (**al-'īd al-kabīr**).

DHANB, pl. **DHUNŪB** and **DHUNŪBĀT** – **Qur'ānic** term.
See **sin**

DHĀT – Philosophical term meaning "essence". In the language of the **falāsifa** it is used in opposition to **wujūd** ("existence").

DHAWQ – "Tasting". For the **Ṣūfīs** it is a synonym for knowing the spiritual world".
See **ma'rifa** and **wajd**

DHAWU'L-ARḤĀM – Expression used in religious law (**fiqh**) to refer to "relatives through the female line", who according to the **school of law** of **Hanbalism** have no rights of succession.
See **'asaba**, **dhū**, **farḍ** and **inheritance**

DHAWU'L-QURBA – "Close relatives" to whom a pious Muslim should "do good" according to a verse in the **Qur'ān**.
See **dhū**

DHIKR – "Remembering". From which comes "repetition" of the name of God or of His **Beautiful Names** "litany". – Liturgical practice used by **Sūfīs** to reach a state of **ecstasy**. The **dhikr** may be performed alone or in a group.

DHIMMA (**pact of**) – "Pact of protection" granting the status of **dhimmī**.

DHIMMĪ – "Tributary" protected according to the rules of the pact of **dhimma** who, in return for this, was bound by various conditions. – Within this legal framework, the non-Muslims included the "People of the Book" (**ahl al-kitāb**) mentioned in the **Qur'ān** (Jews, Christians and even Zoroastrians). These people were allowed freedom of worship provided that they paid the tribute known as **jizya** and accepted an inferior status. They were forbidden to carry arms, ride horses or hold certain administrative posts, and they had to accept the differences in **dress** used to mark their segregation. – Non-Muslims retained their own religious jurisdiction safeguarded within their community but if a dispute arose between one of them and a Muslim, the case was judged by the **qāḍī**. – While a non-Muslim woman could marry a

Muslim, it was not permitted for a Muslim woman to take a non-Muslim husband. – The unequal formulation of this latter statute is attributed to the second **caliph ‘Umar** but it may date from the later period of the **Umayyad** caliph ‘Umar II. It was applied more strictly at some times than others.

DHŪ, pl. **DHAWŪ** – Term meaning “possessor of, endowed with” used in various expressions and a number of personal names.

DHU’L-ḤIJJA – Twelfth **lunar month** of the Islamic **calendar**. Generally qualified by the adjective **ḥaram** or “sacred” since it is the month in which the **ḥajj** takes place.

DHU’L-KIFL – Or Ezekiel. Biblical figure mentioned in the **Qur’ān**.

DHU’L-NŪN – See **Yūnus**.

DHU’L-QA‘DA – Eleventh **lunar month** of the Islamic **calendar**. Generally called **ḥaram** or “sacred”.

DHU’L-QARNAYN – The “two-horned”. In the **Qur’ān**, Alexander the Great, also called Iskandar, is said to have built a wall to prevent Gog and Magog from oppressing the **Banū Isrā’īl**. – From the twelfth century, he became a legendary Islamic hero.

DIETARY LAWS – A number of passages in the **Qur’ān** forbid the eating of certain foods. – Adapted from the rules followed by Jews, most importantly the eating of pork and of animals not killed according to ritual slaughter (**dhabḥ**) is forbidden as is the drinking of wine.

DĪN – The most commonly accepted meaning of this term today is “religion”. – Used in the **Qur’ān** to mean variously “judgement” (see **madīna** and **yawm al-dīn**), “debt, claim, obligation” and “religion” as in the verse “Religion in the eyes of God is Islam” and in various expressions such as “the religion of truth” (*dīn al-ḥaqq*) and “the immutable religion” (*al-dīn al-qayyim*), literally “the religion of **Ibrāhīm**/Abraham. – Used elsewhere to form titles given to princes and then religious figures, particularly jurists (**faqīh**) and **‘ulamā’**.

See **‘ulum al-dīniyya (al-)**

DĪN-I ILĀHĪ – Eclectic **religious movement** created by the Mughal emperor Akbar who reigned over India from 1556 to 1605.

DISSIMULATION – Legal term.

See **taqiyya**

DIVINE ATTRIBUTES – Arabic *ṣifāt*. – Divine qualities derived from the names given to God in the **Qur'ān** such as **raḥmān** "clement", **raḥīm** "merciful", **qādir** "powerful, **'alīm** "most wise", **ḥayy** "living" and **khāliq** "creator" and which together with some others constitute the **Beautiful Names of God** used in **Ṣūfī** rituals. – While the **Mu'tazilites** consider these attributes to be aspects of the divine essence, **traditionalists** attribute to God qualities, including clemency, power and wisdom, that are eternal but distinct from the divine essence. Furthermore, they distinguish between those that God possesses as a result of His essence and those that He possesses as a result of acts such as speech. By thus attempting to attribute to God qualities similar to those of humans, they were accused by the Mu'tazilites and the **Ash'arites** of preaching anthropomorphism (**tashbīh**). – One of the main sources of disagreement concerned the Word of God which, according to the Mu'tazilites, could not be considered eternal and should be considered to be created. This led to endless debates during the Middle Ages as to whether the Qur'ān was **created** or **uncreated**. These debates continued even into the early twentieth century when a supporter of reformism (**islāḥ**), Muḥammad 'Abdūh, drew a distinction between the uncreated text and the words with which it is recited.

See **bilā kayf**, **kalām Allāh** and **ma'nā**

DIVINE BENEVOLENCE, the BENEVOLENT – See **raḥma** and **Raḥmān (al-)**.

DIVINE MERCY, the MERCIFUL ONE – See **raḥīm (al-)**, **raḥma**, **raḥma (jabal al-)** and **raḥmān (al-)**.

DIVINE NAMES – See **Beautiful Names of God**.

DIVINE PUNISHMENT – See **'adhāb** and **'adhāb al-qabr**.

DIVINE TRANSCENDENCE – Vigorously upheld by **Mu'tazilites** who declare that "Nothing resembles Him [God]".
See **ghayb**

DIVINE WILL – See **irāda**.

DIVORCE – Three ways of dissolving a marriage exist, the unilateral repudiation of the wife by the husband and two types of divorce. – With the procedure called **khul'** a woman can obtain an amicable divorce from her husband provided that she renounces any claim to her dowry (**ṣadāq**). Alternatively, if she claims to have been ill-treated, she can apply to the **qāḍī** for a divorce in her favour.

DĪWĀN – "Register". Whence "financial service" and administrative services entrusted, from the earliest centuries of Islam, to official secretaries (**kātib**). – In the Ottoman period, "council of the heads of service" of the central administration.
See **caliph** and **vizir**

DIYA – In law, "monetary compensation" that can be demanded in cases of **murder** in place of retaliation (**qiṣāṣ**).

DOCTORS of the LAW – See **faqīh**, **molla** and **'ulamā'**.

DOCTRINAL AUTHORITY – Does not really exist in Islam. – The task of ensuring that no innovation (**bid'a**) was introduced was exercised by the **caliph** alone, when there was one. If, as occasionally happened, a caliph attempted to impose a doctrine never previously taught, he would find himself opposed by the **'ulamā'** who also claimed to be guardians of the truth. From this, in the ninth century for example, developed the use of the **miḥna**, a "trial" or "inquisition" undergone by traditionalists who opposed the **Mu'tazilite** caliph al-Ma'mūn. – Since the end of the caliphate, in **Sunnī** countries advice is sought when necessary from the grand mufti although his pronouncements are not considered binding.

DOCTRINAL INNOVATION – See **bid'a**.

DOME of the ROCK – Arabic *qubbat al-sakhra*. – Monument in **Jerusalem** built by the **Umayyad caliph** 'Abd al-Malik in 691 in the centre of the precinct of the former Temple known today as **Ḥaram**.– Octagonal in plan with a double ambulatory, its dome covers the area containing a venerated rock believed to be connected with **Muḥammad**'s ascension (**mi'rāj**) to the Seventh Heaven during his Night Journey (**isrā'**).

DONATION – Legal term.

DOWRY – Legal term.

See **ṣadāq**

DOXOLOGY – Prayer of **praise** to God used constantly either orally or in writing consisting, in addition to the **ḥamdala**, of various formulae such as **Allāh akbar** and **al-mulk lillāh** as well as the frequently used **basmala**.

DRESS – In the Middle Ages, people's function and status were apparent from their clothes. The **dhimmīs**, in particular, were obliged to display various distinctive marks of their position while women had to be **veiled**. –Today such customs are gradually dying out except in the case of the pilgrims entering the "sacred territory" (**ḥaram**) at **Mecca** who demonstrate their entry into a **state of holiness or purity** by putting on special garments. The question of the veil worn by women, sometimes all-concealing, sometimes largely symbolic, remains a much-debated and controversial matter. See **burqa'**, **'imāma**, **lithām**, **qalansuwwa** and **chador**.

DRUZES – Extremist **Shī'ite** politico-religious **movement** derived from **Ismā'īlism** which appeared at the beginning of the eleventh century under the **Fāṭimids** and which continues to this day in Lebanon and Syria. – Its founder, al-Darāzī, developed a doctrine making the **caliph al-Ḥākim** the incarnation of the "cosmic intellect" (**al-'aql** *al-kullī*) and replacing the law (**Sharī'a**) with a series of specific commandments.

DU'Ā' – "Personal invocation, prayer of supplication" that may follow the solemn ritual prayer (**ṣalāt**).

DUNYĀ – "Life or world here below".

See **ākhira** and **'ulūm al-dunyāwiyya (al-)**

DYNASTY, **DYNASTIC** – Terms expressing the situation in the Muslim world where the power of the state (**dawla**) is assumed by several generations of one family of **caliphs** or **governors** and then later **sultans** or other **emirs**. – The transmission of power within these groups had nothing to do with the rules of Islam which support the legitimacy of the authority without laying down conditions for its devolution

E

ECONOMICS (ethical) – Arises in Islam from a number of prescriptions derived from the **Qur'ān**. These seek to avoid excessive accumulation of wealth and to protect the poor (**masākīn**): the prohibition in all transactions to lend at interest (**ribā**); –guarantees relating to deeds of **sale**; traders, overseen by the **muḥtasib**, must avoid any kind of fraud; "hoarding" (**iḥtikār**) is condemned; the authorities may not impose fixed rates (**tas'īr**) except in cases of necessity and should respect the price of a specific commodity established in each city according to the so-called law of the **marketplace**.

See **selling**

ECSTASY – The aim of **Ṣūfis** is to attain the ecstasy that defines their mode of existence. – Identified by them with a mystical union with God, certain forms of which are condemned by the **'ulamā'**. – The **successive stages** vary according to master and **brotherhood**.

See **baqā'**, **ittiḥād**, **ittiṣāl**, **jam'** and **wajd**

ELECT (the) – Those received by God into **Paradise** on the Day of Judgement (**yawm al-dīn**). – The expression recurs in the oldest verses of the **Qur'ān**.

See **abrār**, **aṣḥāb al-janna**, **aṣḥāb al-maymana**, **munjiyāt**, **muqarrabūn** and **sābiqūn**

ELEMENTARY SCHOOL – See **kuttāb**, pl. **katātīb**.

EMIGRATION OF MUḤAMMAD – See **hijra**.

EMIGRANTS (the) – See **hijra** and **Muhājirūn**.

EMIR – Arabic *amīr*, "he who commands". The Turkish equivalent is **beg** or *bey*. – Used originally to refer to the head of the community or **caliph**, called the "Commander of the Faithful" (**amīr al-mu'minīn**), – then to the military leaders and provincial governors including the "Chief Commander" (**amīr al-umarā'**), – then to various figures such as the leader of the **ḥajj** caravan (**amīr'al ḥajj**).

See **amara**, **amr** and **ulu'l-amr**

ENDURING (the) – One of the **Beautiful Names of God**.

See **Qayyūm (al-)**

ESCHATOLOGY – Characteristic of the last **sūras** of the **Qur'ān**, the shortest and the oldest, which announce in apocalyptic terms the imminent end of time, the **resurrection** of the dead and the Day of Judgement (**yawm al-dīn**). – Themes taken up in more detail by theologians (**mutakallimūn**), mystics (**Ṣūfis**) and authors of popular stories.

ESOTERICISM – Particularly in **exegesis**.

See **bāṭin**

ESSENCE – Philosophical term.

See **dhāt**

ETERNITY of the WORLD – Affirmed by the **falāsifa** who rejected the idea of the **creation** of the world *ex nihilo*.

See **ḥadath al-'ālam**

EUNUCHS – Arabic *khāṣī* along with other less specific words. – The use of eunuchs in the entourage of rulers, in the army and in families was common during the Middle Ages. – It is believed to have been justified by a verse in the **Qur'ān** authorising women to appear (unveiled) to servants "uninhabited by desire" which would appear to indicate the existence of eunuch servants in the time of **Muḥammad**.

EVIL – Arabic *su'* when meant generally something sent by **Satan**. – Theologians (**mutakallimūn**) who debated the question of whether human actions (**a'māl**) were or were not brought about by God differed in their view of the extent to which

free will implies individual responsibility. – From the point of view of the law (**Sharī'a**), there are two degrees of evil, that which is "forbidden" (**ḥarām**) being punished by a legal sentence (**ḥadd**) while that which is "reprehensible", (**munkar** or **makrūh**), being punished only by the decision of the **muḥtasib**.

See **good**

EVKAF – Turkish word corresponding to Arabic *awqāf*, pl. of **waqf**.

EXAMINATION OF CONSCIENCE – Term used in **Ṣūfism**. See **muḥāsaba**.

EXEGESIS (of the QUR'ĀN) – Arabic **tafsīr**, when referring to a **literal** interpretation which seeks above all the most obvious meaning of words and formulae. – A second type of exegesis, called **ta'wīl**, is practised by **Ṣūfīs** and disciples of a number of **religious movements**, particularly **Shī'ite** movements such as the **Ismā'īlīs** (some of whom were called **Bāṭiniyya**), and involves an esoteric interpretation of the "hidden meaning" (**bāṭin**).

EXISTENCE – Philosophical term.

See **wujūd**

EXISTENCE in GOD – Expression used in **Ṣūfism**.

See **baqā'**

EXPIATION – legal term.

See **kaffāra**

EXTREMISTS – Among **Shī'ites**, see **ghulāt**.

F

FALĀSIFA – Pl. of *faylasūf*, Arabic transcription of the Greek *philosophos*, and which can be translated as "Muslim philosopher". – Influenced by Neo-Platonic philosophy, these scholars applied it to Islamic doctrine, the result being the introduction of ideas that differed significantly from traditional dogma such as the **eternity of the world**. – They were therefore criticised and condemned by theologians (**mutakallimūn**) and jurists (**fāqihs**).

FALSAFA – Arabic for "philosophy". Studied by the **falāsifa** from the time when the works of the Greek philosophers, particularly the Neo-Platonists, were translated into Arabic. This was done mainly at the "House of Wisdom" (**bayt al-ḥikma**) established by al-Ma'mūn in **Baghdad**. – It was criticised for its failure to reconcile Greek concepts with various elements of Muslim doctrine, such as God's **creation** of the world *ex nihilo*, the immortality of the "soul" (**nafs**) and the **resurrection** of the body.

FALSE ACCUSATION of FORNICATION – Legal term.
See **qadhf**

FAMILY of 'IMRĀN – See **āl-'Imrān**.

FAMILY of MUḤAMMAD – See **āl-Muḥammad**.

FANĀ' – "Annihilation of self". **Spiritual state** preparing the **Ṣūfi** for a state of **ecstasy**.

FAQĪH, pl. **FUQAHĀ'** – "Jurist". Specialist in religious law (**fiqh**) that was formulated during the early periods of Islam by the **schools of law**. – Although occupying a prestigious position in society, he receives no pay unless he is a **qāḍī** or teaches in one of the **madrasas** that emerged from the eleventh century onwards and which were institutions with their own financial resources.
See **molla**, **muftī**, **mujtahid** and **'ulamā'**

FAQĪR, pl. **FUQARĀ'** – "Pauper". In Persian *darwīsh*. Word indicating a **Ṣūfi**, sometimes an ascetic (**zāhid**) who has renounced worldly goods and lives above all on the voluntary charity (**ṣadaqa**) of other Muslims.
See **dervish** and **poverty**

FARĀ'IḌ, FARĀ'IḌ ('ilm al-) – Legal terms.
See **farḍ**

FARḌ, **FARĪḌA**, pl. **FARĀ'IḌ** – Word with two different meanings, "prescription" and "share of **inheritance**". – The religio-legal prescriptions linked to worship as mentioned explicitly in the **Qur'ān** and the **Sunna**. These can be divided into those that are an "individual duty", (*farḍ 'ayn*), and those that are a "collective duty", (*farḍ kifāya*). – The "share of inheritance" is decided by the rules of succession as laid down in the **Qur'ān** and elaborated in the "science of inheritance" (*'ilm al-farā'iḍ*) that makes up part of religious law (**fiqh**).

FASĀD – "Disorder, immorality, corruption" that the **community** of Muslims should shun.

FĀSID – Legal term meaning "**altered**, irregular". Whence "null and void".

FĀSIQ – "Criminal, sinner", someone guilty of a serious **sin** other than heresy, Outlawed by the **Khārijites**, such a person is more usually punished by other Muslim groups by a legal corporal punishment (**ḥadd**).

FAST – See **ṣawm**.

FATĀ, pl. **FITYĀN** – "Young man", often famed for **bravery**. – Term used in reference to the **Slavs** of Muslim Spain and equivalent to **ghulām** in the East. – Used of members of the **futuwwa** associations that became popular from the twelfth century.

FATĀWĀ – Pl. of **fatwā**. Used of the "collections" of the texts of a fatwā or consultation that form part of the body of the religious law (**fiqh**).

FATḤ, pl. **FUTŪḤ** – "Success, victory". Term used in the **Qur'ān** of the victories that God secured for the Muslims through interventions and help. Refers particularly to the taking of **Mecca** which constituted the definitive defeat of his enemies by **Muḥammad**; and the great "conquests", which led to the establishment of a Muslim Caliphal Empire and which were described by Arab chroniclers in different works called "Book of conquests" (*Kitāb al-futūh*).

FĀṬIMA – Daughter of **Muḥammad**, generally called **al-Zahrā'**, "the shining one". Wife of his cousin **'Alī** and mother of **al-**

Ḥasan and **al- Ḥusayn**, she died six months after her father whose inheritance she failed to acquire. A number of her **'Alid** descendants were **imāms** or **Shī'ite** political leaders.

FĀṬIMIDS – **Dynasty** of **Shī'ite caliphs** that came to power in 909 in Ifrīqiya, modern-day Tunisia, and then established themselves in Egypt where they ruled until 1171. – Belonging to the **Ismā'īlī religious movement**, they claimed to descend from **Fāṭima**, the daughter of **Muḥammad**, hence their name. From them arose a number of other politico-religious **movements**.

See **Cairo**, **da'ī**, **Druzes**, **Musta'lians** and **Nizārīs**

FĀTIḤA – Introductory **sūra** of the **Qur'ān** consisting of a short prayer. Must be recited several times during ritual prayers (**ṣalāt**) and on various other religious occasions.

FATWĀ, pl. **FATĀWĀ** – "Opinion on a point of law" given by a jurist (**faqīh**) called a **muftī**. – In the medieval period he had no executive powers: if two muftis consulted by a **qāḍī** on a question of the application of religious law (**Sharī'a**) offered opposing advice, the **qāḍī** would choose the solution that he thought best. A number of recorded recommendations have contributed to the body of jurisprudence. – In modern Iran, a fatwā with executive force can be issued by the supreme **āyatallāh**.

See **fatāwā**

FAYLASŪF, pl. **FALĀSIFA** – "Muslim philosopher".

See **falāsifa** and **falsafa**

FEAR OF GOD – **Qur'ānic concept**.

See **taqwā**.

FESTIVALS – These are: – firstly, obligatory festivals such as the "Major Festival", **al-'īd al-kabīr**, and the "Minor Festival", **al-'īd al-ṣaghīr**, occurring on fixed dates in the **Islamic calendar**; – secondly, additional celebrations and popular traditions often connected with the cult of **saints** and gatherings connected with **Ṣūfī brotherhoods**. – Two festivals particular to **Shī'ism** are **'Āshūrā'**, which mourns **al-Ḥusayn**, and the celebration of **Ghadīr Khumm**.

See **isrā'**, **mawlid**, **mawsim**, **laylat al-bara'** and **laylat al-qadar**

FIDĀ'Ī, pl. **FIDĀ** – Arabic word, meaning "he who sacrifices himself" for a cause. Used since the Middle Ages of various extreme groups in the Middle East and the followers of the **Nizārī** sect. In recent times it has referred to groups agitating in Iran between 1943 and 1955, in Egypt in 1950 and 1951 and, more recently, in Algeria and Palestine.

FIFTH – Arabic **khums**. – A fifth share of booty (**ghanīma**) acquired as a result of conquest that, according to the **Qur'ān** was owed to **Muḥammad** and part of which he would then distribute. – Subsequently, the principle ceased to be applied to **land**, considered by the second **caliph** **'Umar** to be the indivisible property of the **community**. – For the **Ismā'īlī Shī'ites**, the fifth part set aside for the leader of the community should apply not only to any booty but also to the income of the faithful.

FIQH – Lit. "understanding of the religious law (**Sharī'a**)". The word is used more specifically to mean "reflection" on the texts of the **Qur'ān** and the Tradition (**ḥadīth**) that led to the formulation of the law and thus refers to the "civil, penal and religious law" resulting from it. – Those who take part in the formulation of the law in the **schools of law** are known as jurists (**faqīh** – pl. *fuqahā'*). They apply various technical procedures such as "reasoning by analogy" (**qiyās**) and "consensus" (**ijmā'**). – Legal treatises include two large sections dealing with: – ritual acts (**'ibādāt**) and – social rules (**mu'āmalāt**).

See **customary law**, **furū'**, **qānūn** and **uṣūl**

FIRDAWS – One of the names of **Paradise** coming from the Arabic transcription of the Greek *paradeisos*, the meaning of which it has retained.

See **janna**

FIRE or FURNACE – Used in the **Qur'ān** to indicate **Hell**.

See **Sa'īr**

FIRQA, pl. **FIRAQ** – Terms referring to the politico-religious **movements** whose members are condemned, either as guilty of **heresy** (**ilḥād**) or as infidels (**kāfir**) by **Sunnī** writers who described them in specialised works called the *Kitāb al-Firaq*. – The list of these movements varies depending on the author and may include groups ranging from the **Mu'tazilites** and the **Imāmīs** to the most "deviant" **Shī'ite** sects. A distinction is often made between: – the "schismatic" sects that continue to form part of the Muslim **community**, including certain Shī'ites, **Khārijites** and Mu'tazilites, and – sects that no longer form part of the community, including extremist Shī'ites (**ghulāt**). – All these movements criticised each other, mutually excluding one another when disputes occurred. These groups can be contrasted with the large mass of Muslims, the Sunnīs (**ahl al-Sunna wa-l-jamā'ā**), their number being a guarantee of **orthodoxy**.

FITNA, pl. **FITAN** – "Disorder, discord, anarchy", considered to be the worst thing to befall the Muslim **community**. – The events following the assassination of the caliph **'Uthmān** in 656 are referred to as the "great fitna".

FIṬR – The breaking of the fast (**ṣawm**). The Arabic name for the "Minor Festival" is **'Īd al-fiṭr** since it marks the end of the fast observed during **Ramaḍān**.

FIṬRA – Used in philosophical and religious language to mean "natural disposition" towards Islam. A **ḥadīth** states, for example, that "all children are born in accordance with the *fiṭra*", which is to say God's plan. Only then, according to theologians, do a child's parents make it a Jew, Christian or Zoroastrian, implying that all children are originally born Muslims.

FIXED RATE – A practice of the **muḥtasib**.
See **tas'īr**

FLOOD – See **Nūḥ**.

FOOD – See **dietary laws** and **ṣawm**.

FORBIDDEN – One of the categories of human actions.
See **ḥarām**

FORNICATION – Punished by a "legal punishment" (**ḥadd**).
See **zinā'**

FRAUD – Condemned by a **Qur'ānic** verse that criticises those who do not give full measure and who will not go to **Paradise**. – The definition of the institution known as **ḥisba** is based partly on this severe attitude towards swindlers or (*mutaffifūn*).
See **economics (ethical)**

FREE CHOICE – Of a **caliph** by the community.
See **ikhtiyār**

FREE WILL – Notion initially introduced as a result of the opposition of the **Qadarites** to the omnipotence of "God's decree" (**qadar**) asserted by the **Jabriyya** in the **Umayyad** period. – The **Mu'tazilites** then claimed that humans possessed the ability to choose between doing **good** or doing **evil**. – At a later date, the **Ash'arites** too were attracted by the idea of free will although they sought to explain it in another manner, through the theory of **iktisāb**.

FREED SLAVE – Arabic *'atīq* or *mukātab*. – The freeing of **slaves** is recommended by the **Qur'ān**. Slave-soldiers, of which there were large numbers from the ninth century onwards, were often freed and promoted to officer rank.
See **mamlūk**.

FRIDAY – Arabic **jum'a**. Word found in a number of expressions relating to the weekly communal prayer (**ṣalāt**), to a Great Mosque (**jāmi'**), and sometimes to particular markets.

FRIDAY MOSQUE – Great Mosque.
See **jāmi'**

FUQAHĀ' – Pl. of **faqīh** ("jurists").

FUQARĀ' – Pl. of **faqīr** "(paupers), **Ṣūfīs**".

FURQĀN – Term derived from Aramaic that appears in the **Qur'ān**, particularly as the title of a **sūra**. The meaning of this term is not entirely clear: "deliverance", hence "salvation", meaning "the Revelation", the Qur'ān, or else "that which distinguishes Muslims from unbelievers".

FURŪʻ – In legal language, "branches", "applications" or "sciences derived from religious law" (**fiqh**), as opposed to **uṣūl** which are the "foundations" of this law.

FUTŪḤ – "**The conquests**".

See **fatḥ**

FUTUWWA – Term derived from **fatā** meaning "young man" to express the "qualities of youth" and hence the "spirit of chivalry". The name was subsequently given to associations formed in the cities of the Islamic East between the tenth and the thirteenth centuries and made up of young men who sometimes indulged in pillaging and at other times brought about order in societies where the rule of law was weak. Some of these associations were linked to **Ṣūfī** movements and were supported by the **ʻAbbāsid caliph** al-Nāṣir who, around 1200, sought to revive Islam through the unification of various different tendencies at the same time as establishing the dignity of his own position.

See **akhīs**

G

GAMBLING – Mentioned in the **Qur'ān**.

See **maysir** and **qimar**

GATEWAY – Arabic **bāb**. Used figuratively, this word can be used as a title. – Constructed in the form of an **īwān**, these entrances have an important role in the organisation and decoration of religious buildings such as **mosques**, **madrasas**, hospitals (**māristān**) and even **mausoleums**.

GENERAL INTEREST – See **istiṣlāḥ**, **Mālikism** and **maṣlaḥa**.

GHADĪR KHUMM – Pool near **Medina** where **Muḥammad** is believed to have pronounced the words making his son-in-law and cousin **ʻAlī** his successor: "He of whom I am the master, so of him is ʻAlī the master". – **Shīʻites** celebrate the anniversary of this event on the eighteenth day of **dhu'l-**

ḥijja with a joyful festival, in contrast to the **Shī'ite** festival of **'Āshūrā'**, commemorating the mourning for **al-Ḥusayn**.

GHAFFĀR (al-), **GHAFĪR (al-)** – "The Indulgent". One of the **Beautiful Names of God**.

GHANĪMA – Booty seized during **battles** and **conquests**. According to the **Qur'ān**, a **fifth** part of this should go to **Muḥammad**, and the rest to the Muslim warriors.

See **lands (status of)**

GHARĪB – "Exiled, expatriated". Technical term used by certain **Ṣūfīs** to refer to someone who has succeeded through divine grace in "exiling himself from himself". – Also used of the Emigrants or **Muhājirūn** among **Muḥammad's Companions**.

GHAWTH – "Help", more especially from God. – It is given as a title to the most important among the hierarchy of **saints**.

See **abdāl**, **abrār** and **quṭb**

GHAYB –"Mystery of divine **transcendence**", the only mystery in the doctrine of Islam.

GHAYBA – "Occultation". The Twelfth **Imām** of the **Imāmīs** who disappeared in Samarra in Iraq in 874 is believed by them to be in a situation of occultation. – During a period of occultation, religious law (**Sharī'a**) is interpreted by the **mujtahids**.

GHAYR MAKHLŪQ – See **"Uncreated" Qur'ān** and **kalām Allāh**.

GHĀZĪ – "He who takes part in a raid, a brief military expedition". – Also has the more precise meaning of "he who takes part in a raid against the infidel" (**kāfir**), referring particularly to the warriors of **jihād**, especially from the thirteenth century onwards, in the areas where the Turks adopted this name in their struggle against the Christians of Byzantium and the Balkans. – *Ghāzī*, also a personal name, became an honorific title adopted by medieval sovereigns. In modern times it was the name taken by the founder of modern Turkey, Atatürk "the Gazi".

GHULĀM, pl. **GHILMĀN** – Military slaves employed in the

Middle Ages in different states of the East to form rulers' bodyguards. They were also called **mamluks**, a term which eventually prevailed from the thirteenth century and became established in the Muslim West.

See **fatā**

GHULĀT – "Extremists". Used of certain **Shī'ites** associated with deviant politico-religious **movements**, some of whom even regard their chosen **imām** as divine.

See **firqa** and **Nusayrīs**

GHUSL – In legal language, "major **ablution**".

GOD'S FORGIVENESS – Arabic *maghfira*. Can be sought by means of various formulae of **istighfār**.

See **Ghaffār (al-)**

GOOD – Notion expressed above all by the adjective **ḥasan** ("good") which corresponds more precisely to the term **iḥṣān**, "acting virtuously". A verse in the **Qur'ān** on **piety** explains that to be good a Muslim should follow the religious observances and behave charitably to fellow Muslims. – The word **ma'rūf** is used for the idea of virtuous behaviour imposed on the community by the institution of **ḥisba** and based solely on the obligations of religious law (**fiqh**).

See **evil**

GOOD or AUTHENTIC – Used of a **ḥadīth**.

See **ṣaḥīḥ**

GOVERNOR – Arabic *wālī* – Representatives of the **caliph** or sovereign responsible for the defence and administration of a province of the **Dār al-Islām**. – Given only limited powers under the first '**Abbāsid** caliphs with no authority over **justice** or control of finances, in later times their power varied from one regime to next. They sometimes even became sovereigns, founding their own **dynasties**.

GRAMMAR – Science practised since the earliest years of Islam that sought to understand and explain the **verses** of the **Qur'ān**.

See **exegesis**

GREAT MOSQUE – See **jāmi‘**.

GUARANTEE – In the legal sense see **damān**, guarantee of safety.

See **amān**

GUARANTEED SHARE – In the laws in **inheritance**.

See **farḍ**

GUARDIAN – Legal term.

See **walī**

H

HĀBIL – Abel. Biblical figure mentioned in the **Qur'ān**.

ḤABŪS – "Entailed property".

See **waqf**

ḤADATH al-‘ĀLAM – In theological language, "contingency of the **world**" considered to have had a beginning.

See **creation** and **ḥudūth**

ḤADD, pl. **ḤUDŪD** – Term meaning "limit" and used in the **Qur'ān** to refer to those "restrictive prescriptions" that are divine in origin. It has come to refer also to the "legal punishments" imposed for: – fornication (**zinā'**) and false accusation of fornication; – the drinking of **wine** (*khamr*); – **theft** (*sāriqa*) and **brigandage** (*qaṭ‘ al-ṭarīq*); – **apostasy**. – These punishments, abolished under the Ottoman state in 1858, are today no longer applied in the majority of Muslim countries with western-style constitutions although they remain in force in those countries adhering strictly to religious law (**Sharī‘a**).

See **mukallaf**

ḤADĪTH – "Utterance" and, more particularly, the "word" attributed to **Muḥammad**. These Traditions, the "sentences" transmitted by the **Companions**, were first gathered together at the beginning of the eighth century. Six of these collections, dating from the ninth century, are considered by **Sunnīs** to be canonical and form the basis of the **Sunna** based on the actions and utterances of Muḥammad. The best known is that by a traditionalist (**muḥaddith**) called al-Bukhārī (died 870). – The text (**matn**) of a ḥadīth is always preceded by the "chain or transmitters" (**isnād**) which makes it more or less reliable or "strong".

See **ḍā'īf**, **ḥasan**, **khabar**, **khabar al-wāḥid**, **mashhūr**, **mutawātir**, **qudsī** and **ṣaḥīh**

ḤAḌRA – In the language of **Ṣūfism**, "divine presence". – Among **Ṣūfīs** it also refers to **dhikr**, ceremonies and other occasions when the litanies are recited.

See **majlis**

ḤĀFIẒ – Lit. "knowing the **Qur'ān** by heart". Word used of those scholars having a thorough knowledge of religious matters, particularly of religious law (**fiqh**) and the Tradition (**ḥadīth**).

ḤĀJAR – Hagar.

See **Ismā'īl**

ḤAJAR al-ASWAD (al-) – See **Black Stone**.

ḤAJAR al-MUSTALAM (al-) – "The Stone that is touched". Another name for the **Black Stone**.

ḤAJJ – "Ritual pilgrimage to **Mecca**", known as the Major Pilgrimage, that all Muslims should complete once in their lives if they are physically and financially able. Takes place every year during the first two weeks of the lunar month to which it gives its name, **dhu'l-ḥijja**. – Pilgrims must perform the following rituals or actions: – enter a state of **holiness or purity** by performing the major **ablutions** and putting on special garments; – repeat the invocation **labbayka**; – travel to the plain of **'Arafat** dominated by the **Jabal al-Raḥma**; carry out the "standing" (**wuqūf**) and perform two of the ritual prayers (**ṣalāt**), those for midday and afternoon; – spend a night in **al-Muzdalifa**; – go to **Minā** to perform the ritual **stoning** of one of the three "pillars of stones", **al-jamarat** *al-'aquba*, and make a **sacrifice**; – have their "hair shaved" (**ḥalq**); – go back to Mecca to perform the circumambulation (**ṭawāf**) of the Ka'ba; – return to Minā to perform the ritual stoning of all three **jamarāt** during the three days of **tashrīq** and then back to Mecca for a final circumambulation after which they come out of the state of **holiness or purity**. – In fact, the ḥajj is a continuation of ancient rituals performed before the arrival of Islam in the sanctuary and **ḥaram** at Mecca which were adopted and transformed by **Muḥammad**. It is interpreted essentially as an element in a **monotheistic** cult that allows believers to obtain **forgiveness** for all their **sins**.

See **dress**, **istighfār**, **ṭawāf** and **'umra**

ḤĀJJ – "Pilgrim" who has carried out the **ḥajj** to **Mecca**.

ḤAKAM al- – "The Judge". One of the **Beautiful Names of God**.

ḤAKAM – "Arbiter". The word *al-ḥakamāni* refers to the "two arbiters" at the meeting at **Adhruḥ**. The resulting decision in favour of Mu'āwiya led to the schism between the **Shī'ites** and **Sunnīs**.

ḤĀKIM, pl. **ḤUKKĀM** – "Judge, assistant to the **qāḍī**" who is himself a judge.

ḤĀL, pl. **AḤWĀL** – "States" of the divine essence according to a belief adopted by certain **Mu'tazilites** to explain the existence of divine **attributes**, a problem that also concerned the **Ash'arites** to some extent. – For **Ṣūfīs** it has the meaning of "ways" or "spiritual states" or "stages" along the way to mystic **ecstasy**.

See **manāzil** and **maqāmāt**

ḤALĀL – In legal language, "permitted". Adjective used particularly of the meat of animals slaughtered according to the rules of religious law. The opposite of **ḥarām**.

See **ḥukm** and **dietary laws**

ḤALQ – Act of "shaving one's hair". Ritual carried out by pilgrims to **Mecca** towards the end of the **ḥajj** to indicate that they are leaving a state of **holiness** or **purity**.

ḤALQA – "Circle" of students or listeners around a master whose teachings they follow.

See **madrasa**, **majlis** and **samāʿ**

ḤAMDALA – Action of "pronouncing or repeating the formula **al-ḥamdu li-llāh**".

ḤAMDU li-LLĀH (al-) – "**Praise** belongs to God". Doxology pronounced at the end of a successful action, frequently used in everyday life in both written and spoken language.

ḤAMMĀM – "Monumental baths" with steam rooms. Type of building, partly continuing antique models, found in every town and indispensable in the daily life of Muslims, particularly since the major ablutions (**ghusl**), were performed here.

ḤAMZA – Paternal uncle of **Muḥammad** who took an active part in defending him against his enemies. He was killed by an Abyssinian slave at the battle of **Uḥud**. – A hero of legendary bravery, stories of his adventures were related in popular novels that appeared in a number of different languages.

HAN – See **khān**.

ḤANAFISM – **School of law** founded by Abū Ḥanīfa (died 767) that spread particularly in Iran and later Anatolia, becoming the dominant school in the Ottoman Empire. – Following the principle of **istiḥsān** ("search for the best solution") and making much use of "personal reflection" (**ra'y**), it espoused views that were often less strict than those of other schools (notably in relation to **marriage** and the drinking of **wine**).

ḤANBALISM – **Legal** and **theological school** founded by Aḥmad ibn Ḥanbal (died 855) noted for its **literalism**, it survives today as **Wahhābism**. It was connected with the development of a **traditionalist** tendency accused of anthropomorphism (**tashbīh**).

HAND of FĀṬIMA – Ornament or jewel popularly believed to have **magic** powers. – Representing a hand, cut out of a sheet of gold or silver metal, like other such talismans it is believed to ward off the evil eye.

ḤANĪF – Follower of the **monotheistic** religion. – Name often given to **Ibrāhīm**/Abraham and then to certain pagans living before the arrival of Islam. Later used in a general sense of all Muslims.

ḤAQĪQA – "Spiritual reality" arrived at, according to **Shī'ites** and various mystics, through the **exegesis** of the **Qur'ān** known as **ta'wīl** ("search for the esoteric meaning". – For certain **Ṣūfīs**, the last **spiritual state** on their "path" (**ṭarīqa**).

ḤAQQ, pl. **ḤUQŪQ** – "Reality, truth". – Firstly in a religious and spiritual sense: God is Truth, hence the personal name 'Abd al-Ḥaqq, "servant of the truth", and the **Qur'ānic** expression **dīn** *al-ḥaqq* ("religion of the truth"). – For **Ṣūfīs**, the real certainty reached through the annihilation of self (**fanā'**). Hence the formula attributed to al-Ḥallāj (a mystic who was condemned and executed in 922): *Anā l-ḥaqq*, "I am the truth". – In legal language it often appears in the plural as "the laws of God" (*ḥuqūq Allāh*), referring to the divine prescriptions contained in the Qur'ān.

ḤARAM – "Sacred territory". Applied to four places: – the area surrounding the **Ka'ba** in **Mecca**, also known as *ḥaram Allāh* or *al-ḥaram al-sharīf*, the "August sanctuary" within which it is forbidden to hunt or bear arms and where non-Muslims may not enter; – the area surrounding the mosque at **Medina**; – the area in **Jerusalem** surrounding the **masjid al-Aqṣā** and the **Dome of the Rock** (*qubbat al-sakhra*), also called *al-ḥaram al-sharīf*; – the area around the tomb of **Ibrahīm**/Abraham, in the town of **Hebron/al-Khalīl**, called *ḥaram al-Khalīl* or "of the Friend [of God]".

ḤARĀM – In legal language, "illicit, forbidden". The opposite of **ḥalāl**.

See **ḥukm**

ḤARAM ALLĀH – "Sanctuary of God". Name given to the **Ḥaram** at **Mecca**.

ḤARAM al-KHALĪL – "Sanctuary of the Friend of God". Name given to the **Ḥaram** in **Hebron**.

ḤARAM al-SHARĪF (al-) – "August sanctuary". Name given to the **Ḥarams** of both **Mecca** and **Jerusalem**.

HAREM and **HAREMLEK** – Turkish words derived from the Arabic **harīm**. The first refers to "the female members of a family" as well as the "apartments where they live" and where only the master of the house and the female servants may enter; – the second refers just to the apartments, the "part of a house reserved for the **women**".

ḤARĪM – See **harem**.

HĀRŪN – Biblical figure mentioned in the **Qur'ān** as a prophet and brother of **Mūsā**/Moses, described as his "helper, assistant" (**vizir**).

ḤASAN – "Good" – In legal language, this adjective is used of certain **ḥadīth** that may be used even though they do not have the reliability of those that are **ṣaḥīḥ**.

See **ḍa'if**, **mashhūr**, **mutawātir** and **qudsī**

ḤASAN (**al-**) – Grandson of **Muḥammad**, second **imām** for the **Twelver Imāmīs** and first for the **Sevener Ismā'īlīs**, he held power after his father **'Alī** for six months before making way in favour of the **Umayyads**. He died eight years later and was buried in **Medina** at the Baqī' cemetery where his tomb was later enclosed and venerated in a mausoleum, now destroyed.

al-ḤASAN al-'ASKARĪ – Eleventh **Imām** of the **Twelver Imāmīs**. He died in 874 at **Samarra** where his tomb is venerated in the mausoleum of the **'Askariyayn** where his father **'Alī al-Hādī** is also buried.

HĀSHIMITES – Descendants of Hāshim, great-grandfather of **Muḥammad** and ancestor of the Banū Hāshim clan of the **tribe** of **Quraysh**. The clan subsequently divided into two branches: the descendants of **'Ali** (**'Alids**) and the descendants of **al-'Abbās** (**'Abbāsids**).

See **naqīb**

HASHĪSHĪ, **HASHĪSHIYYŪN** – Name given to the **Nizārīs**.

See **Assassins**

ḤASHR – Term used in the **Qur'ān** for the "gathering" of humankind on the Day of Judgement (**yawm al-dīn**).

ḤASHWIYYA – Term of unknown origin used to refer to the

anthropomorphic **traditionalists**.

See **Ḥanbalism** and **tashbīh**

HAWĀ – "Passion". Refers not only to the desires condemned by **Ṣūfīs**, but also to the doctrinal errors or "deviations" that characterise the various politico-religious **movements** condemned as **firqa**, pl. **firaq**, by early critics.

ḤAWḌ – "Basin or monumental fountain" in the courtyard of a **mosque** where the ritual **ablutions** are performed. – According to the Tradition (**ḥadīth**), the "basin" where, on the Day of Judgement (**yawm al-dīn**), the **resurrected** will meet **Muḥammad** to seek his intercession (**shafā'a**).

ḤAWWĀ' – The first **woman** (Eve), wife of **Adam**. Biblical figure also mentioned in the **Qur'ān** and commemorated near **Mecca**.

ḤAYY (al-) – "The Living". One of the **Beautiful Names of God**.

HAYYĀ 'ALĀ KHAYR al-'AMAL – "Come to the best work". Additional formula that appears in the **adhān** ("call") to prayer used by the **Shī'ites**: its use is an indication of their dominance in a particular region.

HAYYĀ 'ALĀ l-ṢALĀT – "Come to Prayer". Formula used in the text of the "call" (**adhān**) preceding ritual prayers (**ṣalāt**).

HEART – See **qalb**.

HEBRON – Area in Palestine known as **al-Khalīl** in Arabic because of its connection with **Ibrahīm**/Abraham. In the Byzantine period, a cave here was believed to contain Abraham's tomb as well as, according to Muslim writers, the tombs of **Isḥāq**/ Isaac and **Ya'qūb**/Jacob. The "sacred area" around this venerated sanctuary was called the **Ḥaram al-Khalīl**.

HEGIRA – See **hijra**.

HELL – The destination of the damned, presented in the **eschatological** threats in the **Qur'ān** under various names connected with fire (**nār**).

See **jahannam**, **sa'īr** and **saqar**

HELP (**Divine**) – See **ghawth**.

HELPERS (the) – Included among the **Companions** of **Muḥammad**.
See **Anṣār**

HERESY – An idea partly expressed by the word **ilḥād** ("deviation"), there is not an exact equivalent of "heresy" in Islam since there is no **doctrinal court**. All the politico-religious **movements** categorised by Muslim writers as **firqa** describe any movement opposed to their own as "deviationist". – The term is more generally applied to those who depart from the doctrine professed by the majority, the guarantee of **orthodoxy**, in other words the **Sunnīs** or **ahl al-Sunna wa l-jamā'a**. – **Shī'ites** call any non-Shī'ite **mulḥid** or even "infidel" (**kāfir**).
See **zandaqa**

HEZBOLLAH – See **Ḥizb Allāh**.

ḤIJĀB – See **veil**.

ḤIJR – Part of the sanctuary at **Mecca** close to the **Ka'ba** enclosing a semicircular area in which are the tombs of **Ismā'īl** and his mother **Ḥājar**.

HIJRA – "Emigration" of **Muḥammad** and the first Muslims who left **Mecca** for **Medina**, then called Yathrib. – The date, established by the first **caliph Abū Bakr** as 16 July 622, marks the beginning of the Muslim era and its **calendar**. – *Hijra* is also used of the emigration of Muslims who, in imitation of Muḥammad, leave a hostile land for a region where they settle and from which they will return as conquerors.

ḤIKMA – "Wisdom". Often refers to the wisdom of the authors of antiquity whose works were translated in **Baghdad** at the beginning of the ninth century by order of the '**Abbāsid caliph** al-Ma'mūn in the "House of Wisdom" (**bayt al-ḥikma**). – For the **falāsifa**, it is used to describe the passage of the human soul to perfection. – For **Ismā'īli Shī'ites** it indicates the deep truths of the **Qur'ān** that were taught at the **dār al-ḥikma** in **Cairo**, centre of propaganda (**da'wa**) for the **Fāṭimids**. Here wisdom was understood as synonymous with Ismā'īlī doctrine.

See **ishrāq**

ḤĪLA, pl. **ḤIYAL** – "Legal expedients". – Used by certain jurists (**faqīhs**), particularly **Ḥanafites**, to make alterations to the rules of religious law (**fiqh**).

HILĀL – See **crescent moon**.

ḤIRĀ' – Mountain and cave near **Mecca** where **Muḥammad** is believed to have received his first revelation.

ḤISĀB (**'ILM al-**) "Science of calculation".

See **arithmetic**

ḤISBA – Function of the official known as **muḥtasib** whose job it was, in city life, to "promote good and forbid evil", in Arabic **al-amr bi-l-ma'rūf wa-l-nahy 'an al-munkar**. – In practice, this entailed keeping a watch over public morality and controlling the activities of artisans and merchants.

ḤIZB, pl. **AḤZĀB** – Has various senses in the **Qur'ān**, "group, faction, party" or "section" and was subsequently understood in a number of different ways. They include: – grouping of enemies of the Muslims at the time of the **Battle** of the Trench (**Khandaq**) in **Medina**; – those **Arabs** who **converted** to Islam and rallied to **Muḥammad**; – political party; – lastly, a section of the Qur'ān. From this last sense is derived a word for an office performed by **Ṣūfīs**.

ḤIZB ALLĀH – "Party of God" whose victory, according to the **Qur'ān**, is certain. In recent times, the name has been adopted by an Islamist movement that emerged after the revolution of 1979 in Iran and known in English as Hezbollah.

ḤUDAYBIYYA – Valley near **Mecca** where, in 628, **Muḥammad** bound his troops by an oath of allegiance (**bay'a**) and then concluded a pact with the Meccan leaders by which he agreed to postpone his intention of carrying out the pilgrimage to Mecca in return for a guarantee that this could be undertaken with his **Companions** the following year. – A truce (**hudna**) of ten years was also concluded at this time, although it was not respected by Muḥammad whose attack on Mecca in 629 was crowned with "victory" (**fatḥ**).

See **Riḍwān** (**bay'at al-**) and **Shajara** (**bay'at al-**)

HODJAS – Group of **Shī'ite** Muslims of western India connected to **Nizārī Ismā'īlism**, also widespread in East Africa.

HOLINESS or PURITY (**state of**) – Arabic *iḥrām*, from the verb **aḥrama**. Performed before a **pilgrimage** to **Mecca**, the **ḥajj** or **'umra**. – Consists of various rituals carried out when the pilgrim enters the **ḥaram** at one of the special points of entry (**mīqāt**): major **ablutions**, recitation of **rak'as** and discarding of usual **dress** in favour of special garments made of two pieces of unstitched cloth. – To come out of this state is called **aḥalla**. Various rituals are performed by the pilgrim, usually in two stages, to mark the ending of the ritual restrictions.

See **muḥrim**

HOLY PLACES of ISLAM – "The holy places (**ḥaramayn**) of **Mecca** and **Medina**", known since the Middle Ages and still today as "the two ḥarams". – The title "*khādim* **al-ḥaramayn**" ("guardian of the two ḥarams") has, since 1924, belonged to the king of Saudi Arabia who is responsible for the upkeep of the sanctuaries and the annual organisation of the **ḥajj**.

See **imām al-ḥaramayn**

HOSPITAL – See **māristān**.

HOURIS – **Ḥūr**. Name given in the earliest verses of the **Qur'ān** to the virgin **women** in **Paradise** who will be given as wives to the **elect**.

ḤUBB – "**Love**, friendship".

See **'ishq** and **maḥabba**

HŪD – Pre-Islamic prophet mentioned in the **Qur'ān** believed to have been sent to the **'Ād Arabs**.

HUDĀ – The "right path", the "direction along the right path" indicated by the **Qur'ān**.

See **bushrā**

HUDNA – "Truce, temporary peace", concluded between an Islamic country and a territory belonging to the "territory of war" (**dār al-ḥarb**).

See **Ḥudaybiyya**

ḤUDŪD – "Legal punishments": pl. of **ḥadd**.

ḤUDŪTH – Term used by the **falāsifa** and certain theologians (**mutakallimūn**) meaning "to appear, to come into being".

See **ḥadath al-'ālam**

ḤUJJA – "Proof, argument, legal deed".

See **bayyina**, **burhān** and **dalīl**

ḤUJJAT al-ISLĀM – "Proof of Islam", meaning God's guarantor. For **Shī'ites** this title refers to the **imām**. – Name given to the Twelfth **imām** of the **Imāmīs** and also to the **Fāṭimid** "supreme propagandist" (**dā'ī al-du'āt**) and to the second highest member in the **Nizārī** hierarchy. Used in Iran in recent times of the principal **mujtahid** who became the supreme **ayatollah**. – Was given in the twelfth century as a title to the mystic writer and famous **Sunnī** teacher al-Ghazālī.

ḤUKM, pl. **AḤKĀM** – "Judgement, legal status". – In legal language, "category" qualifying **human actions** (**a'māl**) as anything from "forbidden" to "obligatory". These categories are, in Arabic: **ḥarām**, **munkar**, **mubāḥ**, **mandūb** and **wājib**.

ḤULŪL – "Infusion of the divine into living creatures". Hence "incarnation", a belief that is contrary to the oneness of God (**tawḥīd**). – Certain **Ṣūfīs** have been condemned for declaring that God is present within them when they are in a state of **ecstasy**.

See **ḥaqq**

HUMAN ACTIONS – Arabic **a'māl**. A legal decision applied to an action is called **ḥukm**, pl. **aḥkām**.

See **jabr**, **Jabrites**, **free will** and **Mu'tazilites**

ḤUNAYN (Battle of) – Victory of **Muḥammad** over a hostile Arab tribe that took place in a valley of palm groves not far from **Mecca** shortly after the capture (**fatḥ**) of the town. – The **Qur'ān** mentions it, saying that his victory was attributable to the intervention of God and his legions of **angels**.

ḤŪR – See **houris**.

ḤUSAYN (al-) – Grandson of **Muḥammad** and Third **Imām** of the **Twelver Imāmīs** and Second Imām of the **Sevener**

Ismā'īlīs. He refused to take the oath of allegiance to the second **Umayyad caliph** Yazīd, clashed with the troops of the **governor** of Kufa and was killed at **Karbalā'** in Iraq on the 10th day of **Muḥarram** 680. – Considered by his followers to be a martyr (**shahīd**), his death is mourned every year at the festival of **'Ashūrā'**. His tomb has become a venerated sanctuary, an important religious centre having grown up around it.

HUWA HUWA – "He is He". Formula referring to God recited by **Ṣūfīs** who repeat these words as they enter a state of ecstasy.

See **huwiyya**

HUWIYYA – Philosophical term meaning something close to "ipseity" and formed from the pronoun **huwa** or "he". – For **Ṣūfīs** it means "divine ipseity".

HYPOCRITES – Mentioned in the **Qur'ān**.

See **munāfiqūn**

I

'IBĀDAT – Lit. "acts of religious worship". – The list of these prescriptions makes up the first part of the treatises on religious law (**fiqh**), while the second part deals with "social relations" between Muslims (**mu'āmalāt**). – Obligatory alms (**zakāt**) and legal war (**jihād**) fall into the category of religious obligations that are a direct part of the worship of God and are two of the five "pillars of Islam" (**arkān al-dīn**).

See **'abada**

IBĀḌITES or IBĀḌIYYA – Moderate branch of **Khārijism** emerging around 684 that condemned the "elimination" of non-Khārijites (**isti'rāḍ**). – Persecuted in the East, they became established in North Africa during the Ibāḍite dynasty, the Rustāmids between 776 and 909 and later in Mzab where their descendants are still known by the name of **Mzabites**.

See **Azraqites**, **Najadāt** and **Ṣufrites**

IBĀḤIYYA – "Libertines". Those who dispense with Muslim religious observances (**'ibādāt**).

IBLĪS – From the Greek *diabolos*. Mentioned in the **Qur'ān** as the **angel** who refused to bow before **Adam** and who was then cursed by God but given the power to lead men astray. – Also called **al-Shayṭān** and **al-Rajīm**.

IBN – "Son" or "son of". – Used in the part of a personal name called **nasab** or "filiation".

See **banū** and **personal names**

IBN al-'ABBĀS – Son of **al-'Abbās** and cousin of **Muḥammad**. Said to have been a scholar, he handed down numerous **ḥadīths** (Traditions) that are considered to be particularly "sound".

See **'Abbāsids**

IBN MAJAH – Author (died 887) of one of the six canonical collections of the Tradition (**ḥadīth**).

IBN MUJĀHID – Specialist in **Qur'ānic** readings who wrote a treatise in the early tenth century on the "Seven Admissible Readings".

See **Qur'ān** and **qāri'**

IBRĀHĪM – Abraham. Biblical figure who appears in 25 **sūras** of the **Qur'ān** and is presented as a **prophet** and a **ḥanīf**, the founder of **monotheism**. – He opposed those who worshipped idols and received the order to sacrifice his son, **Isḥāq** or **Ismā'īl** depending on the commentators, who was saved at the last moment. He then went to Arabia where he built the **Ka'ba** in **Mecca** and established the rituals of the **ḥajj**. – Islam is described as the "religion" (**milla**) of Ibrāhīm.

'ĪD al-AḌḤĀ – "**Feast** of sacrifices". Another name for the "Major Festival" (**al-'īd al-kabīr**).

'ĪD al-FIṬR – "Feast of the Breaking of the Fast" (**ṣawm**). Another name for the "Minor Festival" (**al-'īd al-ṣaghīr**).

'ĪD al-KABĪR (al-) – The "Major **Feast**", also called **'īd al-aḍḥā**. Celebrated at the same time as the **ḥajj** to **Mecca** and marked by the slaughtering of an animal (**dhabīha**) in memory of

Ibrāhīm/Abraham, it takes place for most Muslims on the tenth day of the month of **dhu'l-ḥijja**, the Day of **Sacrifice**. – Ritual prayers (**ṣalāt**) consisting of two **rak'as** are performed in the **muṣallā**. – Known by other names in different local languages, for example **büyük bayram** in Turkish.

'ĪD al-ṢAGHĪR (al-) – The "Minor **Feast**", also called **'īd al-fiṭr**. – Celebrated at the end of the Fast (**ṣawm**) of **Ramaḍān** and marked by joyful celebrations and the eating of sweet things. – Accompanied by prayers (**ṣalāt**) performed in the **muṣallā**. – Has different names in other languages, for example in Turkish **küçük bayram**.

'IDDA – In legal language, "period of retreat" that must be observed by a **woman** whose husband has **repudiated** her before she can remarry.

See **marriage** and **mu'tadda**

'ĪDGĀH – Persian word corresponding to **muṣallā**.

IDHN – "Admission" into a **Ṣūfī fraternity**.

IDRĪS – Figure mentioned in the **Qur'ān** as a **prophet** often assimilated with the Biblical Enoch but thought by some to have a connection with those Hellenistic wise men bearing the name Hermes Trismegistos.

IFĀḌA – "Wave". **Qur'ānic** term adopted as a technical term in the pilgrimage, describing the crowded mass of **ḥajj** pilgrims as they rush from one place to another between one ritual ceremony and the next, particularly towards **al-Muzdalifa** after completing the "station" (**wuqūf**) at **'Arafāt**.

See **nafar**

IḤRĀM – From the verb **aḥrama**.

See **holiness or purity (state of)**

IḤSĀN – "Living virtuously". Together with "belief" (**imān**) and "exterior accomplishment" (**islām**) of the various religious observances, it completes the idea of **'ibādāt**. – For **Ṣūfīs**, particularly in modern times, it also has the sense of an interiorisation of the ritual obligations.

See **good** and **ma'rūf**

IḤTIKĀR – In legal language, "hoarding" where vital goods are kept in reserve. Condemned by the Tradition (**ḥadīth**).

See **economics (ethical)**

IḤTISĀB AGHASI – Turkish name for the official policing the **market** and corresponding to the Arabic **muḥtasib**.

See **ḥisba**

ĪJĀB – "Offer". Legal term that must appear in all contracts of **sale** to signify the agreement of the seller.

See **selling** and **qabūl**

I'JĀZ – "Inimitable character" of the **Qur'ān**, regarded as the one miracle performed by **Muḥammad**.

See **mu'jizāt**

IJĀZA – Legal term meaning "authorisation to teach" awarded by a teacher of the religious sciences (**'ulūm dīniyya**) to a student who has attended his "sessions" (**majlis**) along with others in the "circle of listeners" (**ḥalqa**). It may apply to a single work or to a whole discipline. – For the **Ṣūfīs** it refers to the "initiation" of a novice into a **fraternity**.

See **madrasa** and **samā'**

IJMĀ' – "Consensus of Muslims on a matter of religious law (**fiqh**)". Almost all the **schools of law** accept this as a third source of the law, after the **Qur'ān** and the Tradition (**ḥadīth**) on which the **Sunna** depends. – Understood in different ways by different schools: – either meaning the consensus of the **Companions** only, – or referring to the consensus of the **community** in any given period.

See **uṣūl al-fiqh**

IJTIHĀD – "Effort of reflection" in legal matters. – Necessary in order to elaborate precise rules based on the **Qur'ān** and Tradition (**ḥadīth**). These are arrived at in different ways according to the four different recognised **schools of law** through the application of the principles of **istiḥsān**, **istiṣlāḥ** and **qiyās**. – For the **Sunnīs** it is only exercised by the founder of a school who possesses "absolute" *ijtihād* (*muṭlaq*), disciples having only "relative" *ijtihād*. Some scholars have said that since the twelfth century the door of *ijtihād* has remained closed although not all agree with this opinion. – In recent times, supporters of reformism (**iṣlāḥ**) have expressed a wish to "reopen" the door of *ijtihād* and since the end of the nineteenth century a number of reforms have been made, due more to political pragmatism than to a new "effort of reflection". – In **Shī'ite** Iran, jurists called **mujtahid** were believed to be the interpreters of the "hidden" **Imām**.

IKHLĀṢ – "Sincerity, purity". Title of a particularly famous prestigious **sūra** in the **Qur'ān** proclaiming the "oneness of God" (**tawḥīd**).

IKHTILĀF – In the language of religious law (**fiqh**), "divergence of doctrines or points of view" between jurists (**faqīhs**) belonging to different **schools of law**.

IKHTIYĀR – "Free choice". – Principle followed by **Sunnīs** when a new **caliph** is chosen, as opposed to the principle of "testamentary designation" (**naṣṣ**) observed by **Shī'ites**.

IKHWĀN – Pl. of **akh**, "brother", meaning "brother in religion" and used in the **Qur'ān**. – Used of members of certain **Ṣūfī fraternities**.

IKHWĀN (al-) – "The Brethren". Members of a political and religious movement inspired by **Wahhabism** and led by Ibn Sa'ūd in Arabia between 1912 and 1930.

IKHWĀN al-MUSLIMŪN (al-) – The "Muslim Brothers". Politico-religious **movement** established in 1928 in Egypt by Ḥasan al-Bannā', a **traditionalist** who preached a return to the faith of the early Muslims (**salaf**). – After the death of al-Bannā', assassinated in 1949, the Brotherhood rose up against the regime and was implicated in the assassination of Anwar al-Sadat in 1981. It is still active and a son of al-Bannā' lives today in Geneva.

IKHWĀN al-ṢAFĀ' – "The Sincere Brothers". Expression sometimes translated literally as "the Brothers of Purity". – Name of the anonymous authors of an encyclopaedia composed at the end of the tenth century and consisting of 52 treatises. – Influenced by the doctrines of **Ismā'īlī Shī'ites**, the intention of this work is to reveal hidden truths to initiates and bring them to unite with the Universal Soul (**nafs**) that rules the world.

IKRĀH – "Compulsion". Legal term used in a verse of the **Qur'ān:** "There is no compulsion in religion" (*lā ikrāh fi'l-dīn*).

See **makrūh**

IKTISĀB – "Acquisition of actions". Theory that according to the **Ash'arite school of theology** justifies the existence of **free will** in humankind.

ILĀHIYYĀT – "Metaphysics, rational theology". Term used in **falsafa** (philosophy) treatises and Muslim theology (**kalām**).

ILḤĀD – "Deviation", hence "**heresy**", the characteristic of a *mulḥid* pl. *mulāḥida*. – **Qur'ānic** term interpreted in different ways at different periods. – Sometimes understood as "rebellion against authority". – More often associated with the deviant doctrines of certain politico-religious **movements**, sometimes even including materialism or **dahriya**.

See **firqa**

'ILLA – In legal language, "effective cause" which justifies the use of "reasoning by analogy" (**qiyās**).

See **Shāfi'ism** and **fiqh**

ILLICIT – In legal language, one of the categories of human action.

See **ḥarām**

ILLUMINATION – In the language of the **falāsifa**.

See **ishrāq**

'ILM, pl. **'ULŪM** – "Science", meaning principally the science of religion and sometimes the knowledge of the Tradition (**ḥadīth**). – Also used to denote the various secular sciences.

See **fiqh**, **kalām**, **tafsīr** and **'ulūm**

'ILM al-QULŪB – "Science of hearts". One of the definitions of **Ṣūfism**.

IMAGES (prohibition of) – See **aniconism**.

IMĀM – "Guide, leader". Term with a number of different meanings although all deriving from the original sense. – In daily life, applied to the person who leads the ritual prayer (**ṣalāt**) in front of the niche of the **miḥrāb** and whose movements are copied by the faithful behind him: he may be any Muslim, though generally it will be an educated man or important figure who assumes this role, for which he receives no payment. – The direction of prayer being the most important duty of the temporal and spiritual leader of the **community**, from the ninth century the **caliph** assumed the title of *imām*, a title already given by **Shī'ites** to the descendants of **'Alī** who sought to take power and who, according to their followers, possessed superhuman qualities (**'iṣma**). – In a parallel development, *imām* continued to be used in classical Arabic with the general meaning of "person holding authority" in any discipline, secular or religious.

See **faqīh**

IMĀM (**SHĪ'ITE**) – For **Shī'ites**, the title of **Imām** indicates sometimes **'Alī** himself and sometimes the descendants of 'Alī who are considered the only figures worthy of exercising the politico-religious power to which they have laid claim. – They include the Twelve Imāms of the **Imāmīs** and the Seven Imāms of the **Ismā'īlīs**, the majority descendants of **al-Ḥusayn**. In addition to these were the Imāms of the **Zaydis**, chosen from among the **'Alids** on the basis of their merits and not of their direct descent from 'Alī. –The Twelve **Imāms** of the "**Twelver**" **Imāmis** are 'Alī first, followed by **al-Ḥasan** and al- Ḥusayn, '**Ali al-Aṣghar**, **Muḥammad al-Ḅāqir**, **Ja'far al-Ṣādiq**, **Mūsā al-Kāẓim**, **'Alī al-Riḍā**, **Muḥammad al-Jawād**, **'Alī al-Hādī**, **al-Ḥasan al-'Askarī** and **Muḥammad al-Muntaẓar**. The "**Sevener**" Ismā'īlīs recognise al-Ḥasan and al-Ḥusayn as their first Imāms followed by **'Ali al-Aṣghar**, **Muḥammad al-Bāqir**, **Ja'far al-Ṣādiq** and then **Ismā'īl ibn Ja'far** and **Muḥammad ibn Ismā'īl**.

IMĀM al-ḤARAMAYN – ("the **Imām** of the two **Ḥarams**"). Name given to the **Ash'arite** theologian al-Juwaynī who was in **Mecca** and **Medina** for four years in the mid-eleventh century.

See **Holy places**

'IMĀMA, pl. **'AMĀ'IM** – "Turban". Along with the Bedouin **lithām**, turbans were for many centuries the normal headwear for Muslims. The colours varied and were sometimes an indication of social status.

See **dress** and **qalansuwa**

IMĀMATE – Function of the **Imām** in his role as leader of the Muslim **community**. – Theorists have debated whether the choice of sovereign should be by **Sunnī** "free choice", **ikhtiyār**, or by **Shī'ite** "testamentary designation" (**naṣṣ**).

See **caliph** and **Shī'ite imām**

IMĀMBĀRĀ – Building used in eighteenth-century India for the **Shī'ite** ceremonies connected with the Festival of **'Āshūrā'**.

See **ta'ziya**

IMĀMZĀDA – "Descendant of an **imām**". Persian term used of any **'Alid** in **Shī'ite** countries such as Iran whose **tomb** is the object of veneration or "pious visitations" (**ziyāras**).

See **mausoleum** and **mazār**

ĪMĀN – "Faith, quality of the believer (mu'min)" consisting of three elements: – interior acceptance of the content of the profession of faith (**shahāda**); – the verbal expression of this profession of faith; – and respect for the ritual obligations (**'ibādāt**). – The various **schools of theology** give different weight to these obligations that, according to some theologians, might increase or diminish faith. – **Ṣūfīs** distinguish between the belief of ordinary people, based on a passive acceptance, that of the intellectual, based on knowledge (**'ilm**), and lastly that of the righteous which is mystic certitude.

IMĀRA – "Amirate or the function of the **amīr**".

See **dār al-imāra**

IMPECCABILITY – A quality possessed by all **Shī'ite imāms**.
See **'iṣma**

IMPENETRABLE (The) – One of the **Beautiful Names of God**.
See **Samad (al-)**

'IMRĀN – Biblical figure who also appears in the **Qur'ān**.
See **āl 'Imrān** and **Maryam bint 'Imrān**

INCARNATIONISM – Used in the language of mysticism.
See **ḥulūl**

INDIFFERENT – "Neither bad nor good". One of the legal categories qualifying human actions.
See **mubāḥ**

INDULGENT (The) – One of the **Beautiful Names of God**.
See **Ghaffār (al-)** and **Ghāfīr (al-)**

INFALLIBILITY – Quality possessed by all **Shī'ite imāms**.
See **'iṣma**

INFIDEL – "Unbeliever", miscreant, pagan.
See **kāfir**

INHERITANCE – The **Qur'ān** states that any inheritance should be divided into shares (Arabic **farḍ**, pl. *farā'iḍ*) according to precise rules whereby an inheritance may not only pass down the male line (**'asaba**), but also through the female line (**dhāwu'l-arḥam**). The size of the share of particular relatives (for example, the father and the mother) is fixed.

INIMITABILITY of the QUR'ĀN – See **i'jāz**.

INJĪL – Name used in the **Qur'ān** for the Gospel revealed to Christ.
See **kitāb**

INSĀN al-KĀMIL (al-) – "The Perfect Man". – Expression used particularly by a number of **Ṣūfīs** who believe such men to be God's representative on earth, there to ensure the divine salvation of the world. – Some Muslims apply this name to **Muḥammad**.

INSCRIPTIONS – **Arabic** script, regarded as holy as the language of the **Qur'ān**, is used by calligraphers to create beautiful inscriptions on buildings and other objects. They not only record the historical circumstances attached to the construction but also have an apotropaic function. – Muslims are surrounded in everyday life by many inscribed quotations from the **Qur'ān** and the **doxologies**.

See **coinage**

IN SHĀ'ALLĀH – "God willing". Formula much used by Muslims in everyday life each time an event in the future, usually unlikely to come about, is mentioned.

INTENTION – Legal term.

See **niyya**

INTERCESSION – Used in theological language.

See **shafā'a**

INTERPRETATIN of the QUR'ĀN – See **exegesis**, **tafsīr** and **ta'wīl**.

INVOCATIONS – Used in the practice of religion.

See **dhikr**, **du'ā'** and **kunūt**

IQĀMA – Technical term indicating the second "call" (**adhān**) that marks the beginning of prayers (**ṣalāt**).

IQRA' – "Recite". Order that Muḥammad is believed to have received during one of his revelations, telling him to transmit the message that was to become the **Qur'ān**.

IQRĀR – In legal language, "confession, acknowledgement". – An important term since a confession is accepted as proof (**bayyina**) and dispenses with the need for "eye **witnesses**" (**shuhūd**, sing. **shāhid**). – It may lead to the setting out of a written deed (**'aqd**).

IQṬĀ' – Land "torn" from the territory of the State and handed over to military leaders or important officials. At the time of the sultanates, an *iqṭā'* often corresponded to a small principality headed by a prince or **emir**.

See **tenth** and **tīmār**

IRĀDA – "Will". Particularly "God's will", source of the **creation** of the world, seen by some theologians as a continuous process.

See **Ash'arism**

'IRFĀN – "Knowledge of the hidden, gnostic truths".
See **ma'rifa**

'ĪSĀ IBN MARYAM – Name given in the **Qur'ān** to Jesus who appears there as the son of **Maryam**/Mary and as a **prophet** sent by God. – His miraculous conception, his mission and his death are narrated in words not unlike those of the Gospels. However, 'Īsā is described as a "servant of God" (**'abd**) and not the son of God: "The Messiah, 'Īsā ibn Maryam was no more than God's apostle and His Word which He cast to Maryam: a Spirit from Him. Believe in God and His apostles and do not say Three".

'ISHĀ' (**ṣalāt al-**) – "Prayer of the beginning of the night". The fifth prayer of the five obligatory daily prayers.
See **ṣalāt**

ISḤĀQ – Isaac. Biblical figure mentioned in the **Qur'ān** as one of the sons of **Ibrāhīm**/Abraham.

'ISHQ – In the language of mysticism, "love (of God)" in the sense of "ecstatic love".
See **maḥabba**

ISHRĀQ – "Illumination". – In the language of the **falāsifa**, or at least in the eleventh-century writings of Avicenna/Ibn Sīnā, it refers to the knowledge that comes from the illumination of the soul (**nafs**) through the active intellect (**al-'aql al-fa''āl**). – Also used, more precisely, to mean "illuminative wisdom" following a theory, influenced by Neo-Platonism and developed by al-Suhrawardī in the twelfth century, according to which the human soul is able to achieve unity with God through the effects of illumination.

ISKANDAR – Alexander the Great.
See **Dhu'l-Qarnayn**

IṢLĀḤ – "Reformism". Movement originating in Egypt at the end of the nineteenth century, the aim of which was to give new life to Islam by returning to its original form and to the ideas of the "ancients" (**salaf**). – Its representatives sought to achieve these aims in different ways. While Jamāl al-Dīn al-Afghānī mainly opposed British imperialism in India and Egypt, rejecting the influence of western materialism, Muḥammad ʻAbduh (died 1905) set about modernising the teaching given at **al-Azhar** and reforming the legal organisation. Rashīd Riḍā founded the journal **al-Manār**, advocated the restoration of a **caliphate** (abolished in Turkey in 1924) and called for the reopening of the "door of **ijtihād**" in order to change certain aspects of religious law (**fiqh**).

See **salafiyya**

ISLĀM – "Submission to God". – But also "religious practice", required of a believer along with "interior acceptance" (**īmān**) and "living virtuously" (**iḥṣān**).

ISLAMISM – Term used in the nineteenth century to indicate Islam both as a religion and a civilisation. – Recently it has acquired a new meaning of a militant fundamentalist Islam that is **traditionalist**, proselytising and prepared to countenance acts of violence.

ISM – Name given at birth, it is one element of a personal name.

ʻIṢMA – For the **Shīʻite Twelver Imāmīs** and **Sevener Ismāʻīlīs**, "impeccability and infallibility" with which the line of **ʻAlid imāms** are believed to be endowed.

ISMĀʻĪLĪS – Followers of a **religious movement** appearing in 765 as a result of a split within **Imāmī Shīʻism** at the time of the death of the **imām Jaʻfar al-Ṣādiq**. – The Ismāʻīlīs rallied to his deceased son **Ismāʻīl** and to Ismāʻīl's son, **Muḥammad**, the latter being the last and seventh in a line of visible imāms, whence they acquired their name of "**Sevener**" Ismāʻīlīs. At the end of the ninth century, however, a man named ʻUbayd Allāh emerged, declaring himself a descendant of Ismāʻīl and his successor and calling himself **mahdī**. He was to establish the **Fāṭimid** dynasty in Ifriqiyya/Tunisia in 909. At about the same time, other Ismāʻīlīs in the east were involved in the uprisings supporting the politico-religious movement *al-Qarāmita*. – At the end of the Fāṭimid period, Ismāʻīlism split into several different branches some of which survive today. – Influenced by ideas of Neo-Platonism, these groups believe that God gave birth to either a Soul (**nafs**) or to an Intellect (**‘aql**) with which the **imām** had direct communication making him the only interpreter of the law (**Sharī‘a**).

See **Druzes**, **Musta‘lians**, **Nizārīs** and **Qarmatis**

ISMĀ‘ĪL – Ishmael. Biblical figure described in the **Qur’ān** as the son of **Ibrāhīm**/Abraham and **Ḥājar**/Hagar who came to live in **Mecca** where he helped his father build the **Ka‘ba**. – He is also believed by most commentators to be the son whom Ibrāhīm was about to sacrifice, an episode commemorated on the Day of **Sacrifice**.

ISMĀ‘ĪL ibn JA‘FAR – The Sixth **Imām of the Ismā‘īlī Shī‘ites**, he was the son of **Ja‘far al-Ṣādiq**, as was **Mūsā al-Kāsim** who was chosen as Seventh Imām of the **Twelver Imāmīs**. He predeceased his father, dying in 762, but it was recognised that he would be succeeded by his son **Muḥammad ibn Ismā‘īl** who was to be the last imām.

ISNĀD – "Chain of transmission" of the traditions (**ḥadīths**), it can be stronger or weaker depending on the reputation of the successive transmitters cited, going from **Muḥammad** himself to present-day scholars. The degree of reliability attributable to each text (**matn**) is determined by this method.

ISRĀ’ – As described in the **Qur’ān**, the "Night Journey" made by **Muḥammad** from the "Sacred Mosque" (**masjid al-ḥaram**) (understood by all commentators as the sanctuary at **Mecca**) to the "Distant Mosque" (**masjid al-aqṣā**), interpreted either as a celestial sanctuary, hence a kind of "ascension" to the Seventh Heaven (**mi‘rāj**), or as the sanctuary in Jerusalem that came to be known by this name. – The date of the journey was fixed on the 27th day of **Rajab** when it is celebrated each year.

ISRAFĪL – The **angel** who will announce the Day of Judgement (**yawm al-dīn**) by sounding a trumpet for the **resurrection** of the dead.

ISRĀ‘ĪL – Another name for the Biblical figure **Ya‘qūb**/Jacob, mentioned in the **Qur'ān** as a **prophet**.

See **Banū Isrā'īl**

ISRĀ'ĪLIYYĀT – Material of Hebrew origin integrated by commentators into their explanation or **exegesis** of the **Qur'ān**.

ISTIGHFĀR – "Entreaty for **God's forgiveness**". Made particularly during the **pilgrimage** to **Mecca**. – Also present in the entreaties (**du 'ā'**) practised since the early years of Islam and gaining in popularity with the development of **Ṣūfism**.

See **sin**, **Ghaffār (al-)**, **ḥajj** and **'umra**

ISTIṢḤĀB – "Continuation". – Principle used in religious law (**fiqh**) according to which a state of fact continues to exist until such time as the contrary is demonstrated. Secondary notion specific to the **school of law** of **Shāfi'ism**.

ISTIḤSĀN – "Search for the best solution". – Refers particularly to the method used by scholars of the **school of law** of **Hanafism** to resolve practical problems posed by the application of the law (**Sharī'a**).

ISTIṢLĀḤ – Principle used in religious law (**fiqh**) which consists of "taking into consideration the general interest (**maṣlaḥa**)". Method favoured followers of the **school of law** of **Mālikism** to resolve practical problems posed by the application of the law (**Sharī'a**).

ISTINBĀT – "Effort of understanding the deeper meaning" of the **Qur'ān** leading to the "hidden meaning" (**bāṭin**) through **ta'wīl**, a form of exegesis. Term used in the context of a justification for an esoteric approach.

ISTI'RĀḌ – "Elimination of sinful believers". Practice advocated by certain extremist **Khārijites** known as **Azrakites** who broke away from the **Ibāḍīs** and other more moderate branches.

ISTIṬĀ'A – In the language of philosophy, "capacity to act freely". Used particularly by **Mu'tazilites** who affirm the idea of **free will**, stating that humans have the "capacity to obey or not" before acting (*qabla l-fi'l*).

ITHM – "Major sin" that God does not forgive. Only committed through **associationism**.

I'TIKĀF – "Pious retreat in a **mosque**".

I'TIZĀL – The action of "standing apart". – Attitude adopted by **Mu'tazilites** when they refused to pronounce on the position of a "guilty Muslim" who from then onwards was neither really a believer nor an infidel. – The **Mu'tazilites** called the situation of such a person **manzila bayna-l-manzilatayn**.

ITTIḤĀD –A term used by **Ṣūfīs** meaning "mystic union with God" which leads to a state of **ecstasy**.

ITTIṢĀL – Term used in mysticism meaning "**ecstasy** through nearness to God" but without true "union".

ĪWĀN – Architectural element taking the form of a vaulted room enclosed on three sides, the fourth side being open with a monumental arch. Found particularly in **mosques** and **madrasas** from the eleventh century, such spaces formed part of the internal arrangements around a central courtyard and also acted as an entrance **gateway**.

J

JABAL al-RAḤMA – "Mountain of Mercy". Hill dominating the plain of **'Arafat** at the foot of which **ḥajj** pilgrims beg for **God's forgiveness** in the ceremony of the "standing" (**wuqūf**).

JABBĀR (**al-**) – "The Strong". One of the **Beautiful Names of God**.

JABR – "Compulsion". Technical term used in religious law (**fiqh**) and applied particularly to the compulsion that a father can exercise over a prepubescent daughter by giving her in **marriage**: this practice of the law (**Sharī'a**) has recently been abolished in Saudi Arabia. – Used in the language of theology to mean "divine compulsion" over the will and actions of humankind who, according to the **Jabrites**, do not have **free will**. – Also used of a procedure involving the transformation of equations, evidence of the progress made in the science of **arithmetic** in the medieval Muslim world. The word "algebra" is derived from *jabr*.

See **ikrāh**

JABRITES – Followers of a movement espoused in the early years of Islam by **Umayyad** regime which affirmed the existence of "divine compulsion" (**jabr**) on human actions. – Such ideas were opposed by the **Qadarites** but taken up by the traditionalist **Ḥanbalites**.

See **predestination**

JA'FAR al-ṢĀDIQ – The Fifth **Imām** of the **Sevener Ismā'īlīs** and Sixth Imam of the **Twelver Imāmīs**, he was important as a transmitter of traditions (**ḥadīth**), fundamental to Imāmī religious law (**fiqh**) and often called *ja'farī*. – He died in 765 in **Medina** where he was buried and where his tomb was long venerated.

JAHANNAM – One of the names for **Hell**, occurring several times in the **Qur'ān**. Derived from the Hebrew name of a valley in **Jerusalem**.

See **damned**, **nār**, **sa'īr** and **saqar**

JĀHILIYYA – "Days of ignorance", when Islam was not yet known. – The **Ka'ba**, then filled with idols, was already in existence and the pagan pilgrimage rituals performed at **Mecca** were preserved in part in the rituals of the **ḥajj**.

JALĀL – "Divine majesty". Celebrated by many **Ṣūfīs**.

JALĪL (**al-**) – "The Powerful". One of the **Beautiful Names of God**.

JAM' – Mystical term used by **Ṣūfīs** to mean "union with God".

See **ittiḥād** and **ittiṣāl**

JAMĀ'A – "**Community** of the believers". Term similar in meaning to **umma**. – For some authors, however, it has the meaning of the "ancient religion", the only true religion.

See **ahl al-Sunna wa-l-jamā'a**

JAMĀL – "Divine beauty". Celebrated by many **Ṣūfīs**.

JAMARĀT (**al-**) – The "piles of stones" at **Minā** where **ḥajj** pilgrims must carry out the ritual of **lapidation** on the day of

sacrifice and during the three days of **tashrīq**.

JĀMI' – Or *al-masjid al-jāmi'*. Can be translated as "Great Mosque", mosque with a **minbar** or **Friday** mosque. Refers to the monumental building to which all Muslims should come on Fridays at noon for the collective prayers (**ṣalāt**). – The first mosque was set up by **Muḥammad** next to his house in **Medina** and enlarged in the **Umayyad** period. Until about the thirteenth century, there was only one mosque in each area. – Later, the number of mosques multiplied and, in outlying areas of a town, developed into architectural complexes established as **charitable foundations** and including the **mausoleum** of the founder and various public religious buildings such as a college (**madrasa**), library, kitchens for the poor and a hospital (**maristān**).

See **cami**, **masjid** and **masjid-i jum'a**

JANISSARIES – Former **slave-soldiers** who were **freed** after being recruited in the Balkans through the institution called **devşirme**. An army corps of Janissaries was established by the Ottoman sultan Murad I in the fourteenth century,

JANNA – "Garden". – Term generally used in the **Qur'ān** to refer to **Paradise**.

JĀRIYYA – Young **woman**, generally a **slave**. The word acquired the meaning of "**concubine**", since the law (**Sharī'a**) allowed a married man to have slaves as concubines.

See **umm al-walad**

JAWHAR – Lit. "jewel". In the language of philosophy, "substance".

JAWHAR al-FARḌ (al-) – "Atom" susceptible to an "accident" (**'araḍ**) that, according to the theory of some theologians, (**mutakallimūn**) causes it to exist.

See **atomism**

JAZĀ'IR al-ARḌ – "Islands". Name given by **Ismā'īlī Shī'ites** to the regions where their doctrine predominates.

JERUSALEM – al-Quds, the third holy city of Islam. – Conquered in 638, it was then called *Bayt al-maqdis*, "House of sanctity", by analogy with the Aramaic "House of the Temple". The earlier name *Ilyā*, derived from *Aelia*, gradually fell into disuse. Mu'āwiya, the first **Umayyad caliph**, is thought to have been proclaimed there in 660. – By taking possession of the ruined esplanade of the Jewish Temple, Muslims sought to acquire the heritage of the two great monotheistic religions that Islam had come to replace. Traditions developed that were particularly associated with this site and the central "Rock": the ritual prayer (**ṣalāt**) of Caliph **'Umar**, **Muḥammad**'s Night Journey (**isrā'**) and his Ascension (**mi'rāj**). The **masjid al-Aqṣā** and the **Dome of the Rock** were built in the time of the Umayyad caliph 'Abd al-Malik (685–705). In 1009, the **Fāṭimid** caliph al-Ḥākim had the Church of the Holy Sepulchre destroyed, subsequently allowing it to be rebuilt. – The city itself, captured in 1099 by the "Franks" who made it the capital of the Latin Kingdom of Jerusalem until its reconquest by the Muslims in 1187, was temporarily handed over to the Christians between 1229 and 1244 before once again coming under Islamic domination. – At the time of the partition of Palestine carried out by the UN in 1947, the Arab part of Jerusalem, including the Old Town, remained attached to the West Bank. It was occupied in 1967 by the State of Israel but Muslims continue to have possession of the Temple esplanade with its two Islamic sanctuaries.

JEWS – See **Banū Isrā'īl** and **yahūd**.

JIBRĪL – Gabriel. – **Angel** sent to **Muḥammad** to transmit the verses of the **Qur'ān** to him.

JIHĀD – Original meaning, "struggle". – It was used first, in the treatises on religious law (**fiqh**), to mean the "effort of war" that must be waged against infidels (**kāfirūn**) in the name of the law (**Sharī'a**) to ensure the triumph of the true religion. From this comes the meaning of a "legal war", rather than "holy war", decided on by the head of the **community**, that is, by a **caliph** holding the power or by one of his representatives, the **emir** or, later, the **sultan**. – It is therefore a "collective duty” (*farḍ kifāya*) rather than an individual one, intended to ensure the expansion of Islam as a universal religion and creating a state of permanent war with the non-Muslim lands called **dār al-ḥarb**. No lasting peace can be established with such territories, only a sort of truce (**hudna**). – It was the justification for the various armed campaigns extending the limits of the Muslim world beginning, after a series of **battles** and expeditions (**maghāzī**), with **Muḥammad**’s victory (**fatḥ**) over the inhabitants of **Mecca** followed by the great **conquests** of the years immediately after his death. – More or less regularly observed since that time, no jihād has been officially declared since 1914. It has often been undertaken in modern times, however, by independent groups. – Since the tenth century, a number of writers have sought to explain the term as meaning purely defensive war (for example against the Franks and the Mongols) or war against **heresy**. – **Ṣūfīs** have gone so far as to interpret it as referring to the battle against the passions. Hence the expressions “Greater *jihād*” referring to an interior struggle and “Lesser *jihād*” which refers to war.

See **ghāzī**, **mujāhada** and **mujāhid**

JINN – Corporeal beings created, according to the **Qur’ān**, from a flame without smoke. They may enter **Paradise** but can also be condemned to **Hell**.

JIZYA – “Tax” imposed according to the **Qur’ān** on the “People of the Book” or “Possessors of the Scriptures”, the **ahl al-kitāb**. – Later, it became a poll tax exacted from all non-Muslims and distinct from the property tax of **kharāj**. – Now fallen into disuse.

See **dhimmī**

JUDGE – See **qāḍī** and **ḥākim**.

JUDGEMENT of ADHRŪḤ – See **Adhrūḥ** and **ḥakam**.

JUM‘A – **Friday**. The day of prayer (ritual **ṣalāt**) in the Great Mosque (**jāmi‘**).

See **masjid-i jum‘a**

JUMĀDĀ I and II – Fifth and sixth lunar months in the Islamic **calendar**.

JUND – "Army" that assisted the expansion of Islam. – At the period of the great **conquests**, it was composed entirely of Muslim **Arabs** installed in the administrative districts also known as *jund*. – One of the terms used, along with others such as *jaysh*, of the army as a whole. This underwent significant changes over the centuries and eventually consisted mainly of mercenaries and **slave-soldiers** of foreign origin, supplemented by **ghāzīs**, volunteers for **jihād**.

See **Slavs**, **fatā**, **ghulām**, **Janissaries** and **Mamlūk**

JURIST – See **faqīh**.

JUSTICE – Arabic **'adl**. – Notion that does not appear in the theory of religious law (**fiqh**), but the exercise of which is guaranteed by the sovereign or his representative, the **qāḍī**, according to the law (**Sharī'a**). – Those moral treatises (**akhlāq**) that show a strong Aristotelian influence list justice as a virtue. See **dār al-'adl**, **maḥkama** and **maẓālim**.

JUZ' – "Part" of a work. – More specifically, one of the 30 parts into which the **Qur'ān** has been divided to aid memorisation, and distinct from the division into **sūras** and verses (**ayāt**) that were numbered at the time of the rescension and study of the text.

K

KA'BA – Central and essential element around which the sanctuary at **Mecca** was constructed. – A cube with sides 15 metres high and 15 metres wide, it dates from before the advent of Islam but was adopted by **Muḥammad** as a focus of worship, all Muslims being required to face in the direction of Mecca when performing the ritual prayers (**ṣalāt**), and a place of **pilgrimage**. – Known as **bayt Allāh**, "House of God", the **Qur'ān** says that it was built by **Ibrāhīm**/Abraham with the help of his son

Ismā'īl/Ishmael. Various elements related to the Ka'ba are the objects of the pilgrims' invocations or **du'ās** including the **maqām** of Ibrāhīm, the **mustajār**, the **multaẓam**, the **ḥijr**, the **mīzāb**, the **Black Stone** and, not far away, the **Zamzam** well. – The Ka'ba is surrounded by a circular paved area (*maṭāf*) allowing the pilgrims to carry out the ritual "circumambulation" (**ṭawāf**). The esplanade itself, now entirely renovated, was surrounded by porticoes (**riwāq**), constructed in the time of the Umayyad caliph al-Walīd I, marking the boundaries of the "Sacred Mosque" (**al-masjid al-ḥarām**) that lies at the heart of the "Sacred Territory" (**Ḥaram**).

See **kiswa** and **holy places**

KABBARA – Act of pronouncing the formula **Allāh akbar**.

KABĪRA, pl. **KABĀ'IR** – "Major **sin**".

See **ithm**

KAFFĀRA – In the language of religious law (**fiqh**), "expiation" made in cases where the rules governing the **ḥajj** or **ṣawm** have been neglected.

KĀFIR, pl. **KĀFIRŪN, KUFFĀR and KAFARA** – "Infidel, unbeliever, miscreant" or "pagan, idolater" Name given to anyone who does not belong to Islam or who turns away from it by committing the only major **sin**, that of **associationism**. – The practice of **jihād** is directed at these worst of enemies who were obliged to convert or become **slaves**. Christians and Jews, who fall into the category of **ahl al-kitāb**, could seek to benefit from the status of **dhimmī**. – Sinful Muslims have sometimes been called "infidels", especially by the **Khārijites**, as have the followers of deviationist politico-religious movements accused of heresy (**ilḥād**).

See **bid'a** and **firqa**

KAHF – "Cave".

See **ahl al-kahf**

KALĀM – Lit. "discourse, debate". Refers to "Muslim theology" which is a discourse on God, His nature and His **attributes**. – Not accepted by **Ḥanbalite traditionalists** who believe that God is what He has said He is and that therefore such discussion is wrong.

See **schools of theology**

KALĀM ('ilm al-) – "Dogmatic theology".

See **kalām** and **mutakallimūn**

KALĀM ALLĀH – The "Word of God", meaning the **Qur'ān**.

See **divine attributes**, **"created" Qur'ān** and **"uncreated" Qur'ān**

KALĪM ALLĀH – "He who is spoken to by God". Name given to **Mūsā**/Moses from the words in the **Qur'ān**: "God spoke to Moses".

KALIMA – "Word" (of Islam), meaning the "religion of Islam". Synonym of **dīn**.

KARĀMĀT – "Miracles" attributed to a **saint** (**walī**).

See **mu'jizāt**

KARBALĀ' – Place in Iraq where the **'Alid Imām al-Ḥusayn**, son of **'Alī** and considered by **Shī'ites** as the most famous martyr (**shahīd**), was killed. An important town grew up around the mausoleum built over his tomb in the tenth century, attracting many pilgrims.

KARRĀMIYYA – **Religious movement** taking its name from Ibn Karrām (died 869) that spread to Khurāsān and the Middle East. – Its doctrine encouraging asceticism (**zuhd**) also adopted an unusual theological stance in an attempt to overcome the conflict between **Shī'ism** and **Sunnism**.

KASB – "Acquisition of [the rewards and punishments of] actions".

See **iktisāb**

KASHF – Word used in the language of the **Ṣūfīs** meaning "unveiling" of hidden truths.

See **mukāshafa**

KATABA – "To write". A number of words in traditional Muslim vocabulary are formed from this root.

See **kātib**, **kitāb**, **kitāba**, **kuttāb**, **maktab**, **maktūb**

KĀTIB, pl. **KUTTĀB** – "Scribe or secretary" in general and, specifically, the secretaries of the central administration, directing the work of the **dīwāns**. In some periods they exercised important government responsibilities.

See **vizir**

KAYF, **KAYFIYYA** – In the language of philosophy and theology, "modality, analogy".

See **bilā kayf**

KAẒIMAYN (al-) – **Shī'ite mazār** and **mausoleum**, venerated by the **Twelver Imāmīs** in **Baghdad** where the Seventh and Ninth **'Alid Imāms Mūsā al-Kāzim and Muḥammad al-Jawād** were buried. The name soon came to refer to an entire district in the **'Abbāsid** capital.

KHABAR, pl. **AKHBĀR** – "Information, narration" in a general sense. – More specifically "stories of the life of **Muḥammad**". – For **Shī'ites** it also refers to the traditions (**ḥadīths**) going back to their first **Imāms**, particularly **Ja'far al-Ṣādiq**.

KHABAR al-WĀḤID – **Ḥadīth** transmitted by a single person, hence one of only minor value.

See **isnād**

KHĀDIM al-ḤARAMAYN – The "guardian of the two **Ḥarams**".

See **imām al-ḥaramayn** and **holy places**

KHĀḌIR (al-) – Or al-Khiḍr. Figure generally identified with the "servant of God" who appears with **Mūsā**/Moses in a long anecdote in the **Qur'ān**. – In the East he was commemorated by a large number of sanctuaries, the object of pious visitations (**ziyāras**).

KHALAF – "The moderns, successors", as opposed to **salaf** "the ancients, predecessors".

KHALĪFA – **Caliph** or "Successor". – Used first of **Muḥammad's** successors who led the Muslim community. – More generally, it can also mean the deputy of a **qāḍī** or the successor of the founder of a **brotherhood**.

See **Dāwūd**

KHALĪFAT ALLĀH – "**Vicar** of God". Function assigned to **Adam** by God in the **Qur'ān**. – Sovereigns wishing to emphasise the Islamic character of their regimes added the phrase to their titles.

KHALĪL (al-), KHALĪL ALLĀH – "Friend of God". Used of **Ibrāhīm**/Abraham in the **Qur'ān** and giving the modern Arabic name for **Hebron** and its **ḥaram**.

KHALĪQ (al-) – "The Creator". One of the **Beautiful Names of God**.

See **creation**

KHALWA – "Place of retreat" for a **Ṣūfī** practising asceticism (**zuhd**).

KHALWATIYYA – **Ṣūfī brotherhood** taking its name from the mystic 'Umar al-Khalwatī (died 1397) that arose in the Caucasus and spread to Anatolia and the Balkans.

KHAMR – See **wine**.

KHĀN – In Turkish, *han*. "Urban warehouse or isolated caravanserai". Term that in the east replaced the word **qaysariyya**. Word used in the Ottoman period alongside **bedesten**, while in Iran the term **ribāṭ** was still widespread. – These buildings, sometimes the work of the sovereign, brought an economic prosperity regulated by the law (**Sharī'a**) to the Muslim world. Outside the towns they began to spring up along the caravan routes including that taken by **pilgrims** going to **Mecca**.

See **darb al-ḥajj**

KHANDAQ (Battle of) – "**Battle** of the Trench' of 627 when the inhabitants of **Medina** commanded by **Muḥammad** successfully defended the city from attack by soldiers from **Mecca**. – This great success for the Muslims, resulting in the retreat of the attackers, was due largely to their **foresight** in preparing a protective trench on the advice of the Persian Salmān.

KHĀNQĀH – See **monastery**.

KHARĀJ – Heavy "property tax" levied on **lands** captured at the time of the **conquests** and more significant than the obligatory alms (**zakāt**) paid by Muslims. – It was decided by the **Umayyad caliphs** to continue to exact such taxes, regarded as rent on land that was now Muslim property, from conquered landowners even after their **conversion** to Islam. – At a later date, the lands in question were in part given to important figures or military leaders as "fiefs" (**iqṭā'**), subject only to the levying of a tithe justified as being the equivalent of zakāt.

KHĀRIJITES – Followers of **'Alī** who turned away from him in 657, forming their own politico-religious **movement**, when, after the battle of **Ṣiffīn**, he had agreed to abide by the arbitration judgement pronounced at **Adhruḥ** favouring Mu'āwiya as **caliph** rather than him. – Very strict in their views, they believed that a Muslim committing a **sin** should be excluded from the **community** or even executed. They supported the choice of a leader (**imām**) for their community who was the best person without distinction of race or **tribe**, an idea departing from the rule obtaining until then that a caliph must be of the **Quraysh** tribe. – They divided into several branches, one of which survives in North Africa as the **Mzabites** while others can be found in Oman.

See **Azraqites**, **Ibāḍites**, **isti'rāḍ**, **khurūj**, **Najādāt** and **Ṣufrites**

KHĀṢĪ – See **eunuchs**.

KHĀTAM al-ANBIYĀ' – "Seal of the **Prophets**". Name given to **Muḥammad** to emphasise that he was the last in the long line of prophets mentioned in the **Qur'ān**.

KHAṬĪB – "Official preacher" at the Great Mosque (**jāmi'**).

See **khuṭba** and **minbar**

KHATM – Technical term meaning the "complete recitation" of texts such as the **Qur'ān** or a collection of **ḥadīths**.

KHAṬṬ – See **Arabic** (**script**).

KHAYBAR – Oasis in Arabia lying to the north of **Medina** and inhabited by Jewish tribes, captured by **Muḥammad** in 628. – The **land** cultivated by the inhabitants was restored to them on condition that they surrender half their harvest. The tax called **jizya** is based on this precedent. – In 642, the Jews of Khaybar were expelled as were all those who were still living in Arabia.

See **Najrān**

KHIḌR (al-) – See **al-Khaḍir**.

KHIRQA – Arabic name for the garment worn by **Ṣūfīs** made up of patches of woollen cloth. A new member of a **brotherhood** would receive it at the end of his initiation.

KHITĀN – See **circumcision**.

KHIYĀR – In the language of religious law (**fiqh**), "option" or choice of withdrawal allowed to one of the parties in a contract in the period before completion of the bargain.

See **bay'** and **ikhtiyār**

KHIZĀNA – "Library". Particularly those available to the students (**ṭālibs**) of a **madrasa** and consisting almost entirely of donated works on the **religious sciences**.

See **waqf**

KHODJAS – Local name of the **Shī'ites** living in western India descended from the **neo-Ismā'īlīs** or **Nizārīs**.

KHURŪJ – "Sortie, uprising, revolt". – The **Khārijite** politico-religious **movement** took its name from this word.

KHUMS – Used in a technical sense, "**fifth**".

KHUṬBA – "Ritual address" given from the **minbar** on Fridays before the solemn collective prayer (**ṣalāt**), it is both a political speech and a religious sermon. – Always includes a formula of invocation addressed to the leader of the **community**, the **caliph** or, later, the **sultan** or **emir**. In the Middle Ages this reference was the equivalent of a recognition, by a local leader, of the authority of the sovereign and its omission was regarded as an act of rebellion or a declaration of independence.

See **jāmi'** and **khaṭīb**

KINGSHIP of GOD – Or power.

See **mulk lillāh (al-)**

KISMET – Turkish word from the Arabic *qisma*. In the Ottoman period it had the meaning of **maktūb**, "it is written". – Now much used in everyday language.

See **predestination**

KISWA – Silk cloth decorated with pious inscriptions covering the **Ka'ba**. It is renewed each year. – Nowadays made in **Mecca**, it once used to be sent by the sovereign responsible for the protection of the **holy places**, for a long time this being the '**Abbāsid caliph**.

KITĀB – "Book, writing, roll". In the **Qur'ān**, it refers to the list of humankind's good and bad actions that will be laid before God on the Day of Judgement (**yawm al-dīn**). – Also refers, again in the Qur'ān, to the Scriptures of the Jews and the Christians who are called the "People of the Book" (**ahl al-kitāb**). – Later used to mean "The Book", which is to say the Qur'ān, another name for which is **muṣḥaf**.

See **qayyim al-kitāb**

KITĀBA – In the vocabulary of religious law (**fiqh**), the act of **freeing** a **slave** who buys his freedom for an agreed sum payable to his master.

KUBRAWIYYA – **Ṣūfī fraternity** founded by Najm al-Dīn Kubrā (died 1221) that spread particularly to Central Asia.

KÜÇÜK BAYRAM – Turkish name for the "Minor **Festival**" (**'īd al-ṣaghīr**) held at the end of the fast (**ṣawm**) of **Ramaḍān**.

See **büyük bayram**

KUFR – "Impiety, infidelity, disbelief".

See **kāfir**

KUNŪT – "Invocation" that may be recited during ritual prayer (**ṣalāt**). Often a synonym of **du'ā'**.

KUNYA – First part of a male or female **personal name** consisting of either **Abū**, "father of", or **Umm**, "mother of", followed by the real or imaginary name of a son or daughter. – It is polite to address someone using his or her kunya.

See **propriety**

KURSĪ – "Seat or throne of God" mentioned in a verse in the **Qur'ān** known as the "verse of the Throne" (*āyat al-kursī*) that is considered particularly important and appears in many ancient

inscriptions. – Also refers to the stand on which the copy of the Qur'ān recited by a reader in a **mosque** is placed.

See **'arsh**

KUTTĀB, pl. **KATĀTĪB** – Or sometimes *maktab*. "Elementary school" where children learn to read and write using the text of the **Qur'ān**. – Sometimes incorrectly referred to a "Qur'ānic school" whereas the teaching of the Qur'ān is carried out in a **madrasa**.

L

LABBAYKA – "Behold me, O Lord". – Formula recited during the **pilgrimage** to **Mecca** on the path that leads the pilgrim from one of the **mīqāt** of the **ḥaram** to a sight of the **Ka'ba** in the case of the **'umra** pilgrimage or to the plain of **'Arafat** in the case of the **ḥajj**.

LAFẒ – "Utterance", particularly in the expression *al-lafẓ bi-l-* **Qur'ān** ("utterance of the **Qur'ān**"). In an attempt to resolve the problem of the "**uncreated**" or "**created**" **Qur'ān**, a number of writers including al-Ghazali (died 1111) suggested that while the recitation of the Qur'ān was a human creation the text itself remained uncreated.

LĀHŪT – The "world of the divinity".

See **malakūt**

LA'NA – "Curse". Especially God's curse that, according to the **Qur'ān**, will fall on infidels (**kāfirūn**) and those guilty of fraud or lying.

LAND (status of) – Based in principle on the rules laid down in the **Qur'ān** according to two main options. – Land possessed by Muslims in Arabia is subject to **zakāt**, meaning a **tenth** (*'ushr*) as were lands abandoned by the former owners, some of the latter being given to Muslims as **iqṭā'** by the State. – **Caliph 'Umar** did not distribute the lands conquered "by force", however, arguing that they were the property of the **community**. The occupants of these lands continued to pay a rent equal to a heavy land tax levied in former times called **kharāj**.

See **mīrī** and **tīmār**

LAPIDATION – "Stoning". Legal punishment (**ḥadd**) imposed on those committing fornication (**zinā'**). Still enforced in those countries where **Sharī'a** law is strictly observed. – A symbolic ritual stoning is carried out during the **ḥajj** at the "piles of stones" (**jamarāt**) at **Minā** on the Day of **Sacrifice** and the days of **tashrīq**. The *jamarāt* represent **Shayṭān**, **al-rajīm** or **Iblīs**.

LAQAB – "Honorific" name or "sobriquet" added to a **personal name**. – Usage developed above all for sovereigns, the **laqab** becoming the name of the dynasty, or for **emirs**, **'ulamā'** and other prominent figures when the name often incorporated the terms **dawla** (Sayf al-Dawla, for example) or **dīn** (Nūr al-Dīn). – Many different elements were added to such titles.

LAST DAY – Day of Judgement.

See **yawm al-dīn**

LAST JUDGEMENT – See **sā'a** and **yawm al-dīn**.

LAṬĪF al- – "The Benevolent". One of the **Beautiful Names of God**.

LAW – See **fiqh**.

LAWḤ al-MAḤFŪẒ (al-) – "The preserved tablet". – Expression in the **Qur'ān** referring to the eternal text where the entirety of God's revelation is preserved or, more generally, which contains all knowledge.

LAYLAT al-BARĀ'A – "Night of Forgiveness or Repentance". Celebrated on the fifteenth day of **Sha'bān**, particularly in Iran, India and Turkey.

LAYLAT al-QADAR – "Night of Power or Destiny". Night of the 27th day of **Ramaḍān**, marking the anniversary of God's first revelation to **Muḥammad**. – According to popular belief, a person's destiny is fixed on that date each year. Ritual prayers (**ṣalāt**) on this day are particularly well-attended.

LEGAL ACKNOWLEDGEMENT – "Confession".

See **iqrār**.

LEGAL ACT – See **'aqd**.

LEGAL CONSULTATION – See **fatwā**.

LEGAL EXPEDIENT – See **ḥīla**.

LENDING with INTEREST – Legal term.
See **ribā**

LI'ĀN – In the language of religious law (**fiqh**), "**oath** of anathema" permitting a husband to refuse paternity of a child. – Surviving from the pre-Islamic period, it was adopted by Islamic jurists (**faqīhs**) but rarely used.
See **la'na**

LIBRARIES – See **dār al-'ilm** and **khizāna**.

LICIT – Or "permitted". Adjective applied in legal language to human actions.
See **ḥalāl**

LISTENING – One of the adjectives used of God.
See **samī' (al-)**

LITANY – See **dhikr**.

LITERALISM – Widespread tendency in Islam, influencing the **exegesis** of the **Qur'ān** as practised by groups such as the **Hanbalites** and **Wahhābīs**. In an extreme form it can become what has been described as anthropomorphism (**tashbīh**).

LITHĀM – Veil concealing the lower part of the face used by Bedouin. – In modern times it has become one of the attributes of a **saint**.

LIVING (the) – One of the **Beautiful Names of God**.
See **al-Ḥayy**

LOGIC – Philosophical discipline.
See **manṭīq**

LOVE – Does not appear in Muslim thought except in **Ṣūfism** which describes several kinds of love, identifying allusions to them in the **Qur'ān**.
See **ḥubb**, **'ishq**, **maḥabba** and **wajd**

LIGHT – See **nūr**.

LIGHTS – Playing an important role in both official and popular religious ceremonies, they were much used during the Middle

Ages, taking the form of large candles called *shama'*, pl. *sham'*, torches called *mash'al,* chandeliers and oil lamps, generally called *qandīl* or *miṣbāḥ*. This usage led to the production of worked bronze stands to hold the lights and enamelled glass that could reflect the light (*nūr*) of their flames.

LUGHA – See **Arabic** (language).

LUQMĀN – Figure mentioned in the **Qur'ān** as a wise man, his aphorisms are known from early Arabic poetry. He was later numbered among the **Prophets** by some scholars.

LŪṬ – Lot. Biblical figures mentioned in the **Qur'ān** as a **prophet**. – His story is linked to the description of God's punishment (**'adhāb**) that destroyed the "sinful city" identified as Sodom.

LUṬF – "God's goodness or help".
See **Laṭīf (al-)**

M

MABĪT – "Place where one spends the night" during the rituals of the **ḥajj** at **Mecca**, it refers particularly to **al-Muzdalifa**.

MADĀRIS – See **madrasa**.

MADḤ – Text written in praise of a **saint**.
See **manāqib**

MA'DHANA – High place from which the **adhān** ("call" to ritual prayer) or **ṣalāt** is made.
See **minaret**

MADHHAB, pl. **MADHĀHIB** – Lit. "path", "way". In a technical sense it means **school of law**.

MADĪNA – "City" in a general sense. – In earlier times, "place of jurisdiction". The term was originally applied to the place called Yathrib where, after the **hijra**, **Muḥammad** had been received as an arbiter between the various elements of the population. – Later, in the Islamic world, it came to refer to any place where there were figures of authority, **qāḍī**,

muḥtasib and **chief of police**.

See **madīnat al-nabī**

MADĪNAT al-NABĪ – "City of the Prophet" or **Medina**, name given to the town formerly known as Yathrib.

MADĪNAT al-SALĀM – "City of salvation". Name given to **Baghdad**.

See **salām**

MADRASA, pl. **MADĀRIS** – In Turkish, *medrese*, in North Africa *mēdersa*. Establishment devoted to the teaching of religious law (**fiqh**). – Institution created in the East in the eleventh century at the time of the first Seljuq **sultans**. Madāris were private foundations set up by the leading members of government on the basis of a **waqf**, the income from it funding the maintenance of the building, the payments made to the teachers appointed by the founder and, sometimes, board and lodging for students or **ṭālibs**. – Each madrasa was dependent on a particular **school of law**, the first two, founded in **Baghdad** by the vizir Niẓām al-Mulk and by the treasurer were attached to the **Shafiite** and the **Hanafite** schools. – Between the eleventh and thirteenth centuries they spread throughout the East and North Africa. – One of the early aims of the madāris was to defend **Sunnism** against the **Shī'ism** favoured at the time by the **Fāṭimids** in Egypt as well as by various politico-religious **movements** in Syria, Iran and Arabia. The Turkish **amirs**, on the other hand, found it politically advantageous to obtain the support of the **'ulamā'** who taught in them.

MAGHĀZĪ – "Military expeditions" led by **Muḥammad** after the **hijra** once he had become head of the **community** and the Muslim state based in **Medina**. The history of these expeditions was related in a series of works with this title.

See **battles** and **fatḥ**

MAGHRIB (**ṣalāt al-**) – "Sunset prayer". Fourth of the five obligatory daily ritual prayers. Performed immediately after the sun has sunk below the horizon.

See **ṣalāt**

MAGIC – Arabic *siḥr*. Refers to two kinds of magic: natural magic accepted by specialists in religious law (**fiqh**), and demonic magic which is condemned. – Authorised practices, which date from ancient times, are centred around the use of amulets, talismans and other objects bearing apotropaic **inscriptions**. These sometimes take the form of esoteric formulae based on **Arabic script** or numbers and copies of verses from the **Qur'ān**. Popular superstitions often involve seeking blessings (**baraka**) that will ward off the evil eye.

MAḤABBA – "**Love**". – A passage in the **Qur'ān** forms the basis of the **Ṣūfī** doctrine of the reciprocal love between God and the **believer**.

See **ḥubb**, **'ishq** and **maḥbūbiyya**

MAḤBŪBIYYA – In the vocabulary of **Ṣūfism** "the attainment of the rank of those loved by God" (*maḥbūb*). – From this were developed the titles given to the great mystics which often combined the word *maḥbūb* with one of the **Beautiful Names of God**.

See **love**, **ḥubb**, **'ishq** and **maḥabba**

MAHDĪ (al-) – The "well-guided". – Name given to the figure who will come on the Last Day to restore religion after defeating **Dajjāl** (Antichrist). – At various times in history this name has been given to certain reformers, including: – the third **'Abbāsid caliph** al-Mahdī (died 785); – a number of **Shī'ite imāms** including the Twelfth Imām of the **Twelver Imāmīs** who went into occultation in 874, **Muḥammad al-Muntaẓar**; – the "hidden" Imām of the **Ismā'īlī** Shī'ites who manifested himself at the end of the ninth century and founded the **Fāṭimid** dynasty; – the founder of the **Almohad** regime Ibn Tūmart (died 1130); – the founder of the revolutionary movement that emerged in Sudan at the end of the nineteenth century, Muḥammad al-Mahdī (died 1885).

MAHDISM – (*mahdiyya*). Term used to denote the revolutionary movement led in Sudan in 1881 by Muḥammad **al-Mahdī**.

MAḤKAMA – "Court of justice" where the qāḍī adjudicates on disputes between two parties and, through the intermediary of the police (**shurṭa**), hands out legal penalties (**ḥadd**) to those guilty of crimes defined by the law (**Sharī'a**). – In the modern period, the organisation of the judiciary has been modified in most Muslim countries. Tribunals have diversified and are entrusted to specialised magistrates.

MAḤMAL – "Symbolic "palanquin" that the **caliphs** and later the **Mamluk sultans** sent to **Mecca** with each pilgrimage caravan, thus asserting their sovereignty over the **holy places**.

See **amīr al-ḥajj**

MAHR – Gift made by the husband to the wife when a **marriage** is concluded.

See **naqd** and **ṣadāq**

MAJĀZ – "Figurative sense" of certain terms in the **Qur'ān** relating to God, His hand or His **throne** for example. – Applied by the theologians (**mutakallimūn**) opposed to anthropomorphism (**tashbīh**).

MAJLIS – "Session". Term used of: – meetings for the study of the various **sciences**, both religious and profane, – gatherings of **Ṣūfīs** – or **Shī'ite** ceremonies commemorating the death of **al-Ḥusayn** during the festival of **'Āshūrā'**.

See **ḥaḍra** and **samā'**

MAJNŪN – "Madman, possessed, demented". Used of certain **Ṣūfīs** voluntarily assuming a bizarre kind of behaviour.

MĀJŪS – "Zoroastrians". Like the "People of the Book" (**ahl-al-kitāb**), they enjoyed the status of **dhimmī**.

MAKHLŪQ – See **"Created" Qur'ān**.

MAKRŪH – Adjective used in the language of religious law (**fiqh**) of those human actions (**a'māl**) that are "reprehensible but not forbidden". The opposite of **mandūb**.

See **ḥukm** and **munkar**

MAKS, pl. **MUKŪS** – "Taxes," not prescribed by the **Qur'ān** but imposed nevertheless at certain periods on trades and businesses.

MAKTAB – "Elementary school", known more often as **kuttāb**.

MAKTŪB – "It was written". Formula indicating resignation in the face of an unfortunate event.

See **kismet**, **free will** and **predestination**

MALĀ'IKA – See **angels**.

MALAKA – "To possess". Several important terms are formed from the root of this verb.

See **malākūt**, **malik**, **mamlūk**, **milk** and **mulk**

MALĀKŪT – **Qur'ānic** term referring to the "world of realities", intelligible or spiritual, depending on the preferred interpretation, – that of the **falāsifa** – or that of the **Ṣūfīs**.

MALĀMATIYYA – Lit. "those who practise blameworthy actions" (from *malāma*, "blame"). Hence "those who prefer to bring blame onto themselves rather than reveal their high degree of spirituality". – More precisely, certain **Ṣūfīs** who claim to pay no heed to the ritual obligations imposed by the law (**Sharī'a**).

MĀLIKISM – **School of law** identified with Mālik ibn Anas (711–96) following the practice in **Medina** that gave particular importance to the Tradition (**ḥadīth**). It also gave importance to the finding of a solution to particular problems that took account of the "general interest" (**maṣlaḥa**) through the method of **istiṣlāḥ**. – Became widespread particularly in North Africa and in Spain whilst the latter existed. In the East and even in Egypt it retreated before the incoming influence of **Shāfi'ism**. – The most important writer of the school was Saḥnūn (died 854) who lived in Qayrawān.

MAMLŪK – Literally "he who is owned". Hence **slave**. More specifically, "slave-soldiers" recruited by the '**Abbāsid caliphs** from the ninth century onwards in Central Asia to fight in the army (**jund**). They were sometimes **freed** although they remained attached to those who had trained them or who commanded them. – Later, the **sultans** continued to rely on such troops who were to play an increasingly important role both at home and in foreign wars. – The Mamlūk **dynasty**

ruled as **sultans** in Egypt from 1250 to 1517.

See **Slavs**, **fatā** and **ghulām**

MA'NĀ, pl. **MA'ĀNĪ** – "Idea, meaning". – Term sometimes used in theological language in reference to the **attributes** of God.

MANĀQIB – Works written in **praise** of a **saint** or famous **shaykh**.

MANĀR (al-) – "The Lighthouse". Name of a journal founded in **Cairo** in 1899 by Rashīd Riḍā supporting the reformist movement (**iṣlāḥ**).

MANĀRA – Lit. "lantern-tower or lighthouse" where a lamp burns. – Term used later of an essential element in the architecture of a Great Mosque (**jāmi'**). The word passed from Arabic to Turkish, becoming **minaret**.

MANĀSIK al-ḤAJJ – "Rituals of the Major **Pilgrimage**" **ḥajj**.

MANDŪB – Term used in the language of religious law (**fiqh**) of human actions (**a'māl**) that are "recommended but not obligatory".

See **ḥukm**

MANFA'A – In legal language, "usufruct". Used of the enjoyment of any kind of property.

MANHAR – "Place of **sacrifice**" at **Minā** near **Mecca** where the **ḥajj** pilgrims make a sacrifice (**dhabīha**).

See **Ibrāhīm** and **'īd al-kābir (al-)**

MANSŪKH – "Abrogated **Qur'ānic** verse".

See **abrogation**

MANṢŪR (al-) – "The Victorious", thanks to God and His help (*naṣr*). Honorific adopted by several **caliphs** and sovereigns.

MANTLE OF MUḤAMMAD – See **ahl al-kisā'** and **burda**.

MANṬĪQ – "Logic", particularly Aristotelian logic. – Discipline inherited from Antiquity and practised by the **falāsifa** as well as by certain theologians (**mutakallimūn**) and jurists (**faqīhs**).

MANZIL, pl. **MANĀZIL** – In the language of mysticism, "stages" traversed by the soul of a **Ṣūfī** on the way to **ecstasy**.

See **ḥāl** and **maqāma**

MANZILA – "Situation". Term used by the early **Mu'tazilites** in the formula *manzila bayn al-manzilatayn* or "intermediary situation" of an unrepentant sinful believer whom they thought should neither be excluded from the **community**, as the **Kharijites** believed should happen, nor allowed to benefit from those rights reserved for Muslims. But they should be "between the two".

See **i'tizāl**

MAQĀM – Lit., "place where one stands". Used of a monument or place marked by the memory and some physical trace of an ancient **prophet**, usually a handprint or footprint in a rock that has become the object of "pious visits" (**ziyāras**). – The prophet with the greatest numbers of maqāms to his name, both on the route leading from Mesopotamia to Palestine and in Arabia, is **Ibrāhīm**/Abraham whose maqām in **Mecca** is believed to be the stone onto which, according to the **Qur'ān**, he climbed to construct the **Ka'ba** with his son **Ismā'īl**.

MAQĀM MAḤMŪD – "Praiseworthy position", promised to **Muḥammad** in a verse in the **Qur'ān**. – The **Ḥanbalites** interpret this as meaning by God's side, a view disputed by scholars of the **Ash'arite** tendency.

See **tashbīh**

MAQĀMA, pl. **MAQĀMĀT** – In the language of the mystics, "stages" traversed by the soul of a **Ṣūfī** on the way to **ecstasy**.

See **ḥāl** and **manzil**

MAQṢŪRA – "Reserved space" for a sovereign in a Great Mosque (**jāmi'**). – May be marked in the architectural structure of the building but more often indicated by open-work screens in decorated wood.

MARABOUT – In North Africa, both a person regarded as **holy** and a small sanctuary.

See **murābiṭ** and **qubba**

MARKET – Essential element of a town where the rules of ethical **economics** and commerce laid down in the **Qur'ān** must be observed. Traders must, for example, give "full measure" and use "accurate scales". In addition, they must apply the "just price", following the rates established in the town. – The application of these rules is overseen by the **muḥtasib**.

See **bāzār**, **mīzān**, **qaysariyya** and **sūq**

MA'RIFA – "Knowledge," with various different senses depending on context: – act of understanding, – in mystical language, the object of knowledge and intuitive understanding which leads to God and engenders **love**. – **Ṣūfīs** are often called *ahl al-ma'rifa*, "endowed with the understanding of the spiritual world".

See **'ārif**

MĀRISTĀN or **BĪMĀRISTĀN** – "hospital", the first of which was established on the order of **Caliph** Hārūn al-Rashīd (786–809) in **Baghdad** by a Christian doctor from Jundishapur in Iran where an similar institution already existed, set up by the Sasanians. – Others followed, especially in the tenth century, in the capital and the larger towns in the provinces. From the thirteenth century, these buildings developed a characteristic and increasingly attractive architectural form as a result of the increasing numbers of **charitable foundations** endowed by rich patrons.

MARRIAGE – Based on a contract drawn up before two witnesses and sometimes a **qāḍī** between a man and a woman. According to the rules of three **schools of law**, the woman must be represented by a matrimonial **guardian**. – The **Qur'ān** implies that a husband should pay a dowry (**ṣadāq**), sometimes paid in instalments and which remains the property of the woman. The ceremony has no special **religious** ceremony but it is "recommended" that verses from the Qur'ān be recited that day. – The husband, who must support his wife and has authority over her, may, according to a verse in the Qur'ān and so also according to religious law (**fiqh**), marry four wives whom he must treat equally. Today, polygamy is subject to various restrictions but has only been abolished in two countries, Turkey and Tunisia. – In the Middle Ages, a husband could take female slaves (**jāriyas**) as **concubines**, an option that today has no official sanction. – There are three possible ways of terminating a marriage: unilateral **repudiation** by the husband or one of two types of **divorce**. **Shī'ites** allow a form of temporary marriage called **muṭ'a**.

See **mahr**, **nafaqa** and **naqd**

MARTHIYYA – **Shī'ite** funerary poem commemorating the tragic death of **al-Ḥusayn** at **Karbalā'**.

See **'Āshūrā'** and **ta'ziya**

MA'RŪF – Virtuous behaviour that is the job of the **muḥtasib** to ensure and which is described as "recommended" (**mandūb**). –Concerns only exterior behaviour relating to the social and **religious** life of the **community** such as attending prayer (**ṣalāt**) on Fridays, observing the fast (**ṣawm**) during **Ramaḍān**, and trading honestly.

See **economics** (**ethical**) and **good**

MARWA (**al-**) – Hill near the **Ka'ba** in **Mecca**. Pilgrims must run to and fro between it and the hillock of **al-Safa** several times during the rituals of the run (**sa'ī**).

MARYAM bint 'IMRĀN – Mary, the mother of **'Īsā** '/Jesus, called "daughter of **'Imrān**" in the **sūra** in the **Qur'ān** bearing her name. – Mentioned in several passages partially following the accounts of the Annunciation in the Gospels.

MASHHAD [1] – Monument marking the "spot where a person bore witness to his faith in Islam", sometimes by giving his life. Term applied – to the **tomb** of a "martyr" (**shahīd**), – to those **'Alid Imāms** who died a violent death and are considered by the **Shī'ites** to be "martyrs", – to the sanctuaries commemorating or housing the tomb of a **prophet**, a **saint**, a **shaykh** or some other virtuous figure though not necessarily a martyr.

MASHHAD [2] – Place in eastern Iran where the Eighth **Imām**

of the **Shī‘ite Twelver Imāmis**, **‘Alī al-Riḍā**, was buried in 817. He had died in mysterious circumstances after the **caliph**, al-Ma’mūn, had chosen him as his heir presumptive. A place of pilgrimage, his **mausoleum** or **mashhad** became the name used for the town that grew up around it.

MASH‘AR al-ḤARĀM (al-) – “The sacred place of the rituals”. – Site of a sanctuary at **al-Muzdalifa** between **Mecca** and the plain of **‘Arafāt** where, according to the Tradition (**ḥadīth**), **Adam** and **Ḥawwā’**/Eve met and which is now visited by **ḥajj** pilgrims.

MASHHŪR – “Well known”. Adjective used of a tradition (**ḥadīth**) accepted by a large number of scholars (**‘ulamā’**).

See **ḍā‘īf**, **ḥasan** and **ṣaḥīḥ**

MA‘SIYA – “Serious **sin**, revolt, disobedience”.

See **ṭā‘a**

MASJID – Lit. “place of **sujūd** (prostration)”. From this, “oratory, **mosque**”.

MASJID al-AQṢĀ (al-) – The “Far Mosque”. – Arabic name given first to the esplanade of the Temple in **Jerusalem** which is mentioned in the verse in the **Qur’ān** describing **Muḥammad**’s “Night Journey” (**isrā’**). – Restricted later to the Great Mosque (**jāmī**‘) built by the **Umayyad caliphs** ‘Abd al-Malik and al-Walīd not far from the **Dome of the Rock** to the south of the esplanade now called **Ḥaram**.

MASJID al-ḤARĀM (al-) – The sanctuary at **Mecca** around the **Ka‘ba**.

See **ḥajj** and **‘umra**

MASJID al-JĀMI‘ (al-) – “Great Mosque”.

See **jāmi‘**

MASJID-i JUM‘A – Persian name for a Great Mosque, in Arabic **jāmi‘**.

MASJID al-RASŪL – In **Medina**, the “Mosque of God’s messenger” also known as **ḥaram al-madīna**. Rebuilt in the courtyard of **Muḥammad**’s house where, during his life, the **community** would gather for ritual prayer (**ṣalāt**). – Houses his tomb and those of the two first **caliphs**, his **Companions Abū Bakr** and **'Umar**.

MASKĪN, pl. **MASĀKĪN** – The "poor" to whom, according to a verse in the **Qur'ān** defining **piety**, alms should be given.
See **poverty** and **sā'ilūn**

MAṢLAḤA – "General interest". – One of the foundations of religious law (**fiqh**) in the **Mālikite** school.

MA'ṢŪM – "He who has impeccability and infallibility" or **'iṣma**, the attributes of **Shī'ite Imāms**.

MATERIALISM – See **dahriyya**.

MATHNAWĪ – Poems often dealing with mystical didactical themes that influenced the development of **Ṣūfism** and Ṣūfī thought. – The most famous were those composed in Anatolia by Jalāl al-Dīn Rūmī (died 1273), the founder of the **Mawlawiyya brotherhood** or Mevlevis.

MATN – "Text" of a tradition (**ḥadīth**) that must be preceded in the canonical collections by the **isnād** ("chain of transmitters") that make it possible to evaluate its reliability.

MAUSOLEUM – Arabic *turba* (**qubba**). – Constructions built over venerated **tombs**, particularly those of **'Alid Imāms**, of princes and sovereigns and those of **'ulamā'** and **Ṣūfīs** renowned for their holiness. – They became widespread throughout the Muslim world, some forming the centre of vast sanctuaries that became the object of "pious visitations" (**ziyaras**). – The strict **religious movements** have never approved this type of practice. The **Wahhābīs** in Saudi Arabia, for example, demolished all existing mausoleums, forbidding any further such constructions.

MAWLĀ, pl. **MAWĀLĪ** – **Qur'ānic** term with two meanings: firstly, "master, lord", secondly "ally, friend, protégé". – First used, especially in the plural, of those conquered peoples converted to Islam, Arabised "allies" and "clients" of **Arab tribes** whose status posed a problem for the **community**. Not granted equality with the Muslim Arabs and required to pay **kharāj**, a heavier tax than the **zakāt**, their discontent gave rise to upheavals that threatened the **Umayyad caliphate**. The situation became calmer under the **'Abbāsids**. – From the ninth century, the word *mawālī* was used of the former Turkish soldier-slaves who had been freed and had converted to Islam. – By contrast, *mawlā* in the sense of "lord" was used of sovereigns or other revered figures. The expression **mawlāy**, "my lord", a title given in Morocco to a saint (such as Mawlāy Idrīs, the famous Idrīs I) was also used in this region of members of different **dynasties**. – The word **mawlānā**, "our lord", was used in Turkey and Iran to refer to founders of **Ṣūfī brotherhoods** such as Jalāl al-Dīn Rūmī. – The term *mawlā* in the form of **molla** (or mullah in English) is still used today in **Shī'ite** Iran to refer to religious scholars.

MAWLAWIYYA or **MEVLEVIS** – **Ṣūfī brotherhood** founded in the thirteenth century by Mawlānā Jalāl al-Dīn Rūmī (died 1273) in Konya and also known as the brotherhood of "Whirling **Dervishes**". – It developed in Seljuq and later Ottoman Anatolia as well as other parts of the Middle East.

MAWLID – Popular **festival**, marking the anniversary of the birth of **Muḥammad** on the twelfth day of the month of **Rabī' I**, and sometimes condemned by some **'ulamā'**. One of the first times it took place was in 1207 at Irbil in Upper Mesopotamia and its popularity increased thereafter. – The same term, and also **mawsim**, can also refer to celebrations of the birthdays of **saints**.

MAWQIF – Place where pilgrims perform the ritual of the "station" (**wuqūf**) on the **'Arafāt** plain on the first day of the **ḥajj**. – It is indicated by two boundary markers called "signals" (**a'lām**).

MAWQIF al-NABĪ – "Place where the Prophet stood". – Spot close to Mount **'Arafāt** where **Muḥammad** is believed to have stood when addressing the **ḥajj** pilgrims performing the ritual of **wuqūf**.

MAWSIM – Popular **festival**, also called **mawlid**, marking the anniversary of the birth or death of a **saint**. – Often characterised by the gathering of vast crowds particularly if the festival is associated with the activities of a **brotherhood**.

MAWT – See **death**.

MAYSIR – "Game of chance, gambling", a kind of lottery. Forbidden by the **Qur'ān**.

See **qimār**

MAẒĀLIM – "Unjust or oppressive actions". – Name given in the Middle Ages to a special court held only by the **caliph** and distinct from the **justice** exercised by a **qāḍī**. It was intended to "right wrongs" denounced to the person in authority or his representative and thus to control the actions of the **kātibs** ("secretaries") of the administration. It also performed the role of a court of appeal against sentences handed out by the qāḍīs. – At some periods it functioned as a high court trying those accused of **heresy**, the most famous episode being the trial and execution of the **Ṣūfī** al-Ḥallāj in 922. – Its functions were replaced by the institution of the **dār al-'adl**.

See **ruq'a**

MAZĀR – Place visited by pilgrims seeking succour and **blessings** when performing a "pious visitation" (**ziyāra**). Such places might be a **maqām**, a **mashhad**, a **tomb**, sometimes a **mausoleum**, as well as a natural object such as a stone, tree or cave.

MAZĀR-I SHARĪF – "The august place of pilgrimage" or **mazār**. – Town in Afghanistan that grew up around a **mausoleum** identified in the twelfth century as that of **'Alī**. Since then it has continued to be the object of pilgrimage.

MECCA – Arabic *Makka*. Today this town is the religious centre of Islam and the most important of the **holy places** to which crowds of **ḥajj** pilgrims flock each year. It is still forbidden to non-Muslims to enter the "sacred territory" (**Ḥaram**). – The pre-Islamic structure of the **Ka'ba** survives here within the "Sacred Mosque" (**al-masjid al-ḥarām**) mentioned in the **Qur'ān**. – **Muḥammad** was born in this town that owed its prosperity both to trade and its pagan sanctuary. He grew up and first preached his new **monotheistic** religion here, initially without success. He left the city in 622, his emigration to Yathrib/**Medina** being known as the **hijra**. He founded a Muslim state in Medina, returning in triumph to Mecca in 629 after both battles and negotiations. The final conquest (**fatḥ**) of Mecca completed a victory that subsequently embraced the whole of Arabia.

MEDINA – Or *Madīnat al-nabī*, "the city of the Prophet". – Second **holy place** of Islam, its **Ḥaram** surrounding the **masjid al-rasūl** ("mosque of [God's] messenger") containing the **tomb** of **Muḥammad**. – Founded on the site of Yathrib, an oasis 350 km north of **Mecca**, Muḥammad emigrated here, an event known as the **hijra**, and used it as his base in his fight against the people of Mecca. – Once **converted**, the pagan inhabitants of Medina who had called upon Muḥammad to arbitrate in their differences had become known within the new **community** as the "Helpers" (**Anṣār**). The first Muslim state was established here with the so-called "Constitution of Medina" (**ṣaḥīfa**) – The **Jewish** inhabitants of Medina who had rejected the new message were gradually removed, either driven out of the area or even, in some cases, physically eliminated.

MEN of the CAVE – See **ahl al-kahf**.

MESSENGER – Arabic *rasūl,* pl. *rusul* – Name given to the **prophets** sent by God to deliver a message. The last of these is **Muḥammad**, called *rasūl Allāh* ("messenger of God") in the **shahāda**.

See **nabī**

MESSENGER, the – One of the names given to **Muḥammad**.

See **Bashīr (al-)**

MEVLEVIS – See **Mawlawiyya**.

MIDA' – Area attached to many **mosques** with a fountain for minor **ablutions** (*wuḍū*).

See **ḥawḍ**

MIḤNA – "Trial, testing". Term used in reference to the inquisitorial procedures used in the ninth century by the '**Abbāsid**

caliph al-Ma'mūn in an attempt to impose the doctrine of the **Mu'tazilites** and a belief in a **"created" Qur'ān** on the whole population, and especially the **traditionalists**.

See **doctrinal orthodoxy**

MIḤRĀB – Monumental niche in the **qibla**, the back wall of a **masjid**, oratory or Great Mosque (**jāmi'**) in a position to indicate the direction of **Mecca**. – Place where the **imām** stands to lead ritual prayer (**ṣalāt**).

MILK – "Ownership". Religious law (**fiqh**) recognises the right of ownership which is distinguished from *tasarruf* (the right of usage) – Property, land or goods, is subject to various **taxes**, some of which are non-canonical. The right of ownership is limited by the rules of ethical **economics** that forbid "lending at interest" (**ribā**), "hoarding" (**iḥtikār**), and excessive profit-making by traders, whose prices are controlled by the **muḥtasib** through "fixed rates" (**tas'īr**).

MILLA – "Religion". – Sometimes the religion of **Ibrāhīm**/Abraham. – Also refers to the Islamic **community** and sometimes appears as a term synonymous with **umma** and **jamā'a**.

See **millet**

MILLET – Turkish word from Arabic **milla**. In the Ottoman period it was used of the non-Muslim religious communities subject to the ancient status of **dhimmī** but who, at the end of the nineteenth century, acquired new privileges allowing them a greater say in political life.

MINĀ – Valley to the east of **Mecca** on the road to **'Arafāt** where several ceremonies of the **ḥajj** are performed. – After the day of the **wuqūf** at 'Arafāt, pilgrims make a sacrifice here, remembered all over the Muslim world during the festival of **'īd al-kabīr**. This is followed by the ritual **lapidation**s of the most important of the three "pillars of stones" (**jamarāt**), which are stoned later, during the three days of **tashrīq**.

MINARET – Turkish form of Arabic **manāra** and also called **ma'dhana** and **ṣawma'a**. – Today it refers to the tower of a Great Mosque (**jāmi'**) from which the **adhān** (call to prayer) is made. – In earlier times it had other functions: – a lighthouse in the **ribāṭs** by the seashore or on desert routes (the literal meaning of *manāra* being "site of a light"), – tower providing shelter for pious individuals seeking refuge from the world, – tower erected by a sovereign to celebrate his victories.

MINBAR – "Pulpit" with several steps found in a Great Mosque (**jāmi'**) near the **miḥrab**. – Used by the official preacher (**khaṭīb**) for the address (**khuṭba**) made at the beginning of **Friday prayer** (**ṣalāt**).

MĪQĀT – "Point of entry" of pilgrims entering the "sacred territory" (**Ḥaram**) at **Mecca** in order to complete the **ḥajj** or **'umra**. They then enter the state of **ritual purity** marked by the putting on of special garments after performing the major **ablution**. – There are several *mīqāt*, corresponding to what were once the different caravan routes taken by pilgrims, the **darb al- ḥajj**. The entry closest to Mecca was used particularly by the inhabitants of the city.

MIRACLES – See **i'jāz**, **karāmāt**, **mu'jizāt** and **saint**.

MIRACLES of the SAINTS – See **karamāt**.

MI'RĀJ – Lit. "ladder". Name given to **Muḥammad**'s "ascension" on his steed **Burāq**, from **Mecca** or **Jerusalem** into the Seventh Heaven where God commanded him to institute the five daily prayers (**ṣalāt**). He is believed to have placed his foot on the rock (al-sakhra), subsequently venerated in the **Dome of the Rock**. – The account of the *mi'rāj* as related by **Ibn al-'Abbās** expands on the verse in the **Qur'ān** mentioning the **isrā'** ("Night Journey").

MĪRĪ – Turkish term used from the Ottoman period to indicate those **lands** belonging to the State Treasury occupied by Muslim or Christian tenants who benefited from the profits on the land in exchange for the payment of a tax.

MISCREANT – Or "infidel".

See **kāfir**

MIṢR, pl. **AMṢĀR** – The modern Arabic name for Egypt, the name comes from the word for a garrison town established at the time of the great **conquests**, examples being Basra, Kufa, Fustat and Qayrawān.

MĪTHĀQ – "Pre-eternal pact" established, according to the **Qur'ān**, between God and the sons of **Adam** who acknowledged God as their Lord. Also called "Covenant".

MĪZĀB – "Gutter" leading away the water on the roof of the **Ka'ba**. Believed to confer divine blessings on pilgrims who make invocations (**du'ā**s) here.

MĪZĀN – "Balance". Appears in the **Qur'ān** as the instrument used for the "weighing of actions" (**wazn al-a'māl**) on the Day of Judgement (**yawm al-dīn**). Also used in the **Qur'ān** to refer to merchants' scales. **Fraud** is condemned while honesty in trading is ensured by the **muḥtasib**.

MOSQUE FURNISHINGS – See **bisāṭ**, **dakka**, **kursī**, **lights**, **maqṣūra**, **minbar** and **carpet**.

MODERNISM – Tendency found among some Muslim thinkers at the end of the nineteenth century, particularly in India and Egypt, which sought to bring the religious and legal customs of Islam more closely in line with western ideas. – A number of pragmatic reforms were introduced in the areas of family and penal law, going further in some countries than others. It met with opposition from the reformist movement (**iṣlāḥ**) that advocated a return to the teachings of the early Muslims (**salaf**).

MOLLA – Or mullah. Persian name, derived from the Arabic **mawlā**, used by **Shī'ite Twelver Imāmis** for a cleric. The equivalent among Arab **Sunnīs** is the **'ālim** (pl. **'ulamā'**).

MONASTERY – The building housing members of a **brotherhood** formed around a **Ṣūfī** master is generally known as **khānqāh**, a Persian word in origin but which spread throughout the East in the eleventh and twelfth centuries, except in Turkey where the word **tekke** was used. – Earlier, the Arabic word **ribāṭ**, used particularly to describe a small fort occupied by warriors in the holy war (**mujāhidūn**), quickly came to refer to a kind of hostel for religious guests.

– The term **zāwiya** was more common in the Muslim West, referring originally to the place where an **ascetic** withdrew and where his disciples came to consult him.

MONASTICISM – Arabic **rahbāniyya**. Condemned by a tradition (**ḥadīth**) which says: *lā rahbāniyyata fi'l-islām*, "no monasticism in Islam". However, a verse in the **Qur'ān** referring to this subject is more ambiguous. – Various kinds of monasticism developed in Islam at the time of the formation of **Ṣūfī brotherhoods**.

MONISM – Philosophical theory.

See **waḥdat al-wujūd**

MONOTHEISM – Considered by Muslims to be one of the central distinctive features of Islam with its strict belief in "the oneness of God" (**tawḥīd**). – A concept that posed some problems for theologians (**mutakallimūn**), when discussing the **attributes** of God. – Islam rejected the positions held by **Jews** and **Christians** whom it accuses of **taḥrīf** ("alteration") of the archetypical monotheism of **Ibrāhīm**/Abraham, the **ḥanīf**.

MONTH – The Muslim **lunar hijrī calendar** has twelve months of 28 days: **Muḥarram**, **Ṣafar**, **Rabī' I** and **II**, **Jumādā I** and **II**, **Rajab**, **Sha'bān**, **Ramaḍān**, **Shawwāl**, **Dhu'l-qa'da** and **Dhu'l - ḥijja**.

MOON – According to the **Qur'ān**, one of the "signs of God" (**āyāt**). The pre-Islamic **Arab calendar**, regulated according to the movements of the moon, was adopted by **Muḥammad** with a few modifications including the abolishing of the intercalatory days.

See **crescent moon**, **ṣalāt al-kusūf** and **sun**

MORALITY – A concept not defined in religious law (**fiqh**) that only recognises the "legal categorisation" (**ḥukm**) of human actions. – Has a role in the teachings of thinkers influenced by the notion of **akhlāq** (character "traits") and by certain recommendations in the **Qur'ān** as well as by foreign ideas. – One of the main concerns of **Ṣūfism**.

See **economics** (**ethical**)

MOSQUE – Word derived from the Arabic **masjid** which came into European language through Spanish *mesquita.* – "Place in which ritual prayer (**ṣalāt**) is performed", including both the obligatory daily prayer and the superogatory prayer called **nawāfil**. – A distinction is made between a ordinary mosque (private oratories, local mosques with no **minbar** and oratories forming part of another building) and the "Great Mosque" (**jāmi'**) where the solemn Friday prayer and **khuṭba** take place.

MOVEMENTS, POLITICO-RELIGIOUS – A number of these politico-religious movements, called **firqa** in Arabic and sometimes translated as "sect", have been the cause of many disagreements and sometimes schisms as a result of their deviating (**ilḥād**) from the **orthodoxy** of the **Sunnīs**, the **ahl al-Sunna wa-l jamā'a**.

MU'ĀDH ibn JABAL – One of the scribes who wrote down in the lifetime of the Prophet the verses of the **Qur'ān** which he recited.

See **Ubayy ibn Ka'b** and **Zayd ibn Thābit**

MU'ĀMALĀT – "Social rules" that make up the second part of any treatise on religious law (**fiqh**) and following the "acts of worship" (**'ibādāt**).

MUBĀḤ – In the language of religious law (**fiqh**) this term is used to categorise those **human actions** (**a'māl**) that are "neutral".

See **ḥukm**

MUBĀHALA – "Procedure of reciprocal cursing" or trial by ordeal intended to extract the truth. – Proposed by **Muḥammad** in 630 to the Christian leaders of **Najrān** but rejected by them in favour of a guarantee of protection by Muḥammad.

MUEZZIN – From the Arabic *mu'adhdhin.* Person who recites or chants five times a day from a high place, often the top of a minaret, giving the "call" (**adhān**) to the ritual prayer (**ṣalāt**).

MUFTĪ – "Jurist (**faqīh**) who issues legal decisions called **fatwās**" on practical problems for which the treatises on religious law (**fiqh**) have no precise answer. – For a long time he held neither official position nor executive power to back up his decisions. – In the Ottoman Empire, by contrast, a body of paid muftīs was organised in the same way as the **qāḍīs**. They were considered to be of higher rank, under the authority of the **Shaykh al-Islām** who was also known as the "Grand Mufti". He nominated the qāḍīs and sometimes issued fatwās allowing the **sultan** to make changes to the law.

See **qanūn**

MUḤADDITH – "Traditionist", a scholar specialising in the study of the Tradition (**ḥadīth**).

MUHĀJIRŪN – "Emigrants" – **Companions** of **Muḥammad** who followed him when he left **Mecca** to go to Yathrib/**Medina** and who became, with the **Anṣār** ("Helpers"), members of the new **community**. – They included members of **Muḥammad's family**, members of the **Quraysh** tribe and ordinary people.

See **hijra**

MUḤAMMAD – Founder of Islam who was born in **Mecca** into the **Quraysh** tribe and who began to preach a new **monotheistic** religion around 615, as God's "Messenger"(**rasūl**), through the "recitation" of verses (**āyāt**) inspired by God. These were subsequently collected in the **Qur'ān**. – Faced with the refusal of the people of Mecca to convert, he left his city in 622, an event known as the "Emigration" (**hijra**), and went to Yathrib/**Medina** where he established himself as religious, political and military leader. Defeating his enemies in a series of **battles**, he was also successful in negotiating the conquest (**fatḥ**) of Mecca in 629. – Having integrated the clans of the Quraysh tribe into the Muslim **community**, he died in Medina in 632.

MUḤAMMAD al-BĀQIR – The Fourth **Imām** of the **Sevener Ismā'īlī Shī'ites** and the Fifth Imām of the **Twelver Imāmī Shī'ites**. – Famed for his wisdom in matters of religion, he died in 732 in **Medina** where he was buried and where his **tomb** was long held in veneration.

MUḤAMMAD ibn ISMĀ'ĪL – The Seventh and last visible **Imām** of the **Sevener Ismā'īlī Shī'ites**.

MUḤAMMAD al-JAWĀD – The Ninth **Imām** of the **Twelver Imāmī Shī'ites**. He died in 835 in **Baghdad** where he was buried near the **tomb** of his ancestor, the Seventh Imām, **Mūsā al-Kāẓim**. – The two men are venerated by **Shī'ites** in the sanctuary of the **Kaẓimayn**.

MUḤAMMAD al-MUNTAẒAR – Also known as **al-Mahdī**. The Twelfth and last **Shī'ite Imām** of the **Twelver Imāmīs** who went into occultation (**ghayba**) in 874 in **Samarra**. – He disappeared in an underground cellar (***sardāb***) accessible to modern visitors through the sanctuary of the **'Askariyayn**.

See **ṣāḥib al-zamān**

MUḤAMMAD al-TAQĪ – See **Muḥammad al-Jawād**.

MUḤARRAM – First **month** of the Islamic year and often called *mubārak*, "blessed". – The **Shī'ite** day of mourning, **'Āshūrā'**, commemorating the death of **al-Ḥusayn**, falls on the tenth day of this month.

MUḤĀSABA – In the language of mysticism, "examination of conscience". This practice reflects the **Ṣūfīs'** concern with **morality**.

MUḤKAM – Term used to describe those verses of the **Qur'ān** whose meaning is "clear and well-established".

See **exegesis** and **mutashabbih**

MUHLIKĀT – "**Sins** that will lead to perdition" according to the interpretation of mystical writers such as al-Ghazāli (died 1111).

See **munjiyāt**

MUḤRIM – "Having taken the *iḥrām*". Said of a pilgrim in a state of **ritual purity** when performing the **ḥajj** or **'umra** in **Mecca**.

MUḤTASIB – "Magistrate enforcing the **ḥisba**" and the regulation of urban life, both in the Middle Ages and in the strict interpretation of some modern-day Islamicists. – It is his duty to watch over **tradesmen**, preventing fraud, hence his name of "guardian of the markets". He also regulates public morality and religious practices, ensuring the "promotion of the good" (**al-amr bi-l-ma'rūf**).

See **iḥtisāb aghası**

MUJĀHADA – In the language of mysticism, "spiritual effort". One of the "stages" through which a **Ṣūfī** passes on the "path" (**ṭarīqa**) to the attainment of a state of **ecstasy**.

See **ḥāl**, **jihād**, **manzil** and **maqāma**

MUJADDID – "Reviver of Islam", believed to appear at the beginning of every century. – The name was used in India of Aḥmad Sirhindi (died 1624) who was believed to have ushered in the second millennium of the era of the **hijra**.

See **tajdīd**

MUJĀHID, pl. **MUJĀHIDŪN** – "Warriors of the **jihād**". Expression frequently used in the Middle Ages at the time of wars against infidels (**kāfirs**). – Adopted in modern times by members of armed Islamicist groups.

See **fidā'ī**, **ghāzī** and **murābiṭ**

MU'JIZĀT – "Miracles" attributed to the **prophets** as distinct from **karāmāt** performed by the **saints**.

See **i'jāz**

MUJTAHID – "Jurist (**faqīh**) practising **ijtihād**", one of those who founded the **schools of law** and drew up the treatises on religious law (**fiqh**). – Thereafter, until the twelfth century, they confined themselves to laying down the applications (**furū'**) of religious law. – In **Shī'ite** Iran, "interpreters of the religious law (**Sharī'a**) in the name of the "Hidden" **Imām**". – In the nineteenth century, the jurists known as mollas formed a priestly class headed by a "supreme mujtahid", the **ḥujjat al-islām**, later replaced by the supreme **ayatallāh** who still today practises ijtihād in the name of the Twelfth Imām, **Muḥammad al-Muntaẓar**.

MUKALLAF – In legal language, "responsible". A legal sentence (**ḥadd**) may only be imposed on a person who is responsible.

See **taklīf**

MUKĀSHAFA – In the language of mysticism, "understanding" of the spiritual world reached through "unveiling".
See **kashf** and **ma'rifa**

MULḤID, pl. **MULĀḤIDA** – "Rebel, heretic".
See **ilḥād**

MULK LĪ-LĀH (al-) – "The power" or "kingship is God's". – **Doxology** frequently reproduced and repeated in religious **inscriptions** on objects and buildings.

MULTAZAM – "Place of the accolade". Section of the wall of the **Ka'ba** in **Mecca** where pilgrims crowd together during the ritual of the circumambulation (**ṭawāf**).
See **mustajār**

MU'MIN, pl. **MU'MINŪN** – "Believer" in the religion of Islam. – The equivalent of **Muslim** with which it is often associated in the **Qur'ān**, though with no clear distinction between the two terms. – Came to be used frequently as a form of honorific.
See **amīr al-mu'minīn**, **īmān**, **islām** and **umm al-mu'minīn**

MUNĀFIQ, pl. **MUNĀFIQŪN** – "Hypocrites": term used of those citizens of **Medina** who had **converted** to Islam but who maintained links with unbelievers and who are condemned in the **Qur'ān**.
See **riyā'**

MUNJIYĀT – "Qualities required of the future **elect**" as set out by mystical authors such as al-Ghazāli (died 1111).
See **muhlikāt**

MUNKAR – Term used in the language of religious law (**fiqh**) to describe those human actions that are "reprehensible" but not formally "forbidden" by the **Qur'ān**. The prevention of such actions, mainly certain kinds of behaviour in social life, is the job of the **muḥtasib**.
See **ḥukm**

MUQARRABŪN – Those "close" to God". – Mentioned in the **Qur'ān** and referring to the **elect** in **Paradise**.

MURĀBIṬ, pl. **MURĀBIṬŪN** – "Occupants of a **ribāṭ**" or defensive fortress on the frontier. By extension, "soldier of the **jihād**" and equivalent of **mujāhid**. – Still with the sense of "People of the ribāṭ", it can refer more specifically to members of the **Almoravid dynasty**. – Later, in North Africa and particularly in Algeria, a **saintly** person or **marabout**, a name also given to a little sanctuary where the saint is venerated and to the guardian of the sanctuary.

See **qubba**

MURDER – Sometimes justifies a right to legal retaliation (**qiṣāṣ**).

See **diya** and **tha'r**

MURĪD – "Disciple" of a **Ṣūfī** master. – "Novice" in a **Ṣūfī brotherhood**.

MURĪDIYYA – **Ṣūfī brotherhood** founded in 1888 in Senegal by a member of the **Qādiriyya**.

MURJITES – **School of theology** that, in the early years of Islam, refused to exclude from the **community** those who were guilty of serious **sins**, justifying this with reference to the "divine decree" (**qadar**) which determined human actions. – This argument was used particularly to excuse sins committed by the **caliphs** of the **Umayyad** period.

See **predestination**

MURSHID – "Spiritual leader, teacher, master", used particularly by **Ṣūfīs**.

MŪSĀ – Moses. Called **Kalīm Allāh**, "the one addressed by God". – Biblical figure mentioned in the **Qur'ān** as a prophet and "messenger" (**rasūl**) and the subject of several edifying stories. – There is also mention in the Qur'ān of his "servant", identified as **al-Khaḍir** or al-Khiḍr.

MŪSĀ al-KĀẒIM – The Seventh **Imām** of the **Twelver Imāmis**, he died in 799 and was buried in **Baghdad** where his **tomb** was venerated by **Shī'ites**. – Around this developed the sanctuary known as the sanctuary of the **Kāẓimayn** (the "two Kāẓims"), Mūsā and his grandson, the Ninth imām **Muḥammad al-Jawād**, who is buried alongside him.

MUṢALLĀ – Known in Iran as **namāzgāh** and in India as **‘īdgāh**. – Area in the open air set aside for the ritual prayer (**ṣalāt**) at times of large gatherings of worshippers, particularly for the “prayers of the two festivals” (**ṣalāt al-‘īdayn**).

MUṢAWWIR (al-) – “The Organiser”, he who gives form to things. One of the **Beautiful Names of God**.

MUSHĀ‘ – In legal language, “undivided, joint ownership” when speaking of property (**milk**). A situation that frequently arises on account of the complicated rules of **inheritance**.

MUṢḤAF – “Book” made up of bound sheets. Whence “The Book”, the **Qur’ān**.

MUSHRIK, pl. **MUSHRIKŪN** – Someone guilty of “shirk” (**associationism**), regarded as a **sin** in Islam. Whence the use of the word to mean “infidel” for which the usual term is **kāfir**.

MUSIC – Arabic *mūsīqā* or *musīqī*. Condemned by the strict jurists or **faqīhs**, particularly the **Ḥanbalites** and the **Mālikites**. – Religious music is tolerated, however, especially at popular **festivals** some of which are connected with the veneration of **saints**. It is difficult to draw a line between what is religious music and what is secular.

MUSLIM, pl. **MUSLIMŪN** – “He who surrenders to God”. Often associated with the word **mu’min** in the **Qur’ān**.

See **amīr al-muslimīn** and **islām**

MUSLIM – Author of one of the six canonical collections of the Tradition (**ḥadīth**), he was born in Nishapur in Iran, and died in 873.

MUSLIM CREDO – Profession of Faith.

See **‘aqīda**

MUSLIM CULT – Arabic **‘ibādāt** and **arkān al-dīn**.

MUSLIM HEADWEAR – See **‘imāma**, **lithām**, **qalansuwwa** and **veil**.

MUSTAḌ‘AFŪN – Lit. “the humbled”. Mentioned several times in the **Qur’ān** which promises them salvation. – Commentators have interpreted the term as meaning either the “oppressed” or the “weak”, meaning the poor people of **Mecca** who were unable to accompany **Muḥammad** at the time of the **hijra** (Emigration).

MUSTAJĀR – "Place where protection is implored" between two of the corners of the **Ka'ba** in **Mecca**. Pilgrims stop here during the ritual of circumambulation (**ṭawāf**).

See **multazam**

MUSTA'LIANS – Branch of **Ismā'īlī Shī'ites** who recognised the **Fāṭimid caliph** al-Musta'lī reigning in Egypt from 1094 to 1101 as their **Imām**. In 1142, al-Musta'lī's grandson was declared "hidden" and his representative settled in the Yemen. The Musta'lians later transferred to India where they were known as **Bohoras**.

MUSTA'MIN – "Beneficiary of a guarantee of protection" (**amān**).

MUṬ'A – In the language of religious law (**fiqh**), "temporary **marriage**" permitted in **Shī'ism**.

MUTABARRAK – "Bearer of a **baraka**" (blessing bestowed by God).

MU'TADDA – In the language of religious law (**fiqh**), "woman in the period of **'idda**" after **repudiation** by her husband or after his death.

See **marriage**

MUTAFFIFŪN – "Those committing fraud".

See **fraud**

MUTAKALLIMŪN – Theologians practising dialectic (**kalām**), justifying certain points of dogma through the application of reasoning (**'aql**).

See **schools of theology**

MUTASHABBIH – Term used of those verses in the **Qur'ān** whose meaning is considered to be "ambiguous".

See **exegesis** and **muḥkam**

MUTAWAKKIL (al-) – "He who has faith in God". Term related to the pietistic and mystical notion of **tawakkul**. – Used as an honorific for an **Abbasid caliph** (died 861) who sought to break with the position held by his **Mu'tazilite** predecessors.

MUTAWĀTIR – Term applied to a tradition (**ḥadīth**) relying on a sufficiently large number of transmitters to allow it to be considered "authentic" or "true".

See **dā'if**, **ḥasan**, **mashhūr**, **qudsī** and **ṣaḥīḥ**

MU'TAZILITES – Followers of a politico-religious **movement** set up at the end of the **Umayyad** period (beginning of the eighth century) and characterised by the role it gave to reason (**'aql**) in the interpretation of doctrine. – The first leaders were Wāṣil ibn 'Aṭā and 'Āmr ibn 'Ubayd, while the most important were those at the beginning of the ninth century, Abu'l-Hudhayl, al-Naẓẓām and Bishr. Their beliefs stressed: the "Oneness of God" (**tawḥīd**) and hence the rejection of divine **attributes** and a belief in the **"created" Qur'ān**, – "divine justice" (**'adl**) implying human **free will**, – divine rewards and punishment implying the impossibility of any kind of intercession (**shafā'a**) on the Day of Judgement (**yawm al-dīn**), – the "intermediate position" (**manzila bayna'l-manzilatayn**) of the sinful Muslim, -- the obligation to "promote virtue" (**al-amr bi-l-ma'rūf**). The **'Abbāsid caliph** al-Ma'mūn imposed this doctrine on all his subjects, obliging **traditionists** and jurists to submit to a kind of inquisition called the "trial" (**miḥna**) that continued to be used under succeeding caliphs until the advent of **al-Mutawakkil** in c. 850.

MUTMA'INNA – "Peaceful", used of the soul (**nafs**). – Term used in the **Qur'ān**. – Later entered the vocabulary of the **Ṣūfīs** and was used in the definitions of the three aspects of the **nafs** given by mystical writers such as al-Ghazali (died 1111).

MUTTAQŪN – "The "pious men" who will enter paradise as promised in the **Qur'ān**.

See **muqarrabūn**, **ṣāliḥūn** and **taqwā**

MUWAḤḤIDŪN – The "supporters of the oneness of God (**tawḥīd**)". – The Arabic name for a politico-religious **movement** that took power in the western Maghrib in the twelfth century, founding a **dynasty**. Also known as **Almohads**.

MUWALLADŪN – Name given to **converts** to Islam in Muslim

Spain from the eighth century. Their status was similar to that of the **mawālī** in the East.

MUZDALIFA (al-) – Valley near **Mecca** between **'Arafāt** and **Minā** traversed by **ḥajj** pilgrims. – Pilgrims spend a night here after the **wuqūf** ("station") and visit the **mash'ar al-ḥarām** ("sacred place of rituals").
See **mabīt**

MYSTIC – The first manifestations of mysticism, inspired by verses in the **Qur'ān** evoking the **love** existing between God and humankind, appeared in the eighth century. – The basis of **Ṣūfism** which developed from the ninth century and saw the emergence of **brotherhoods**.

MYSTIC UNION – **Ṣūfīs** attempt to achieve this when they enter a state of **ecstasy**.
See **baqā**, **fanā'**, **ittiḥāl**, **ittihād**, **ittiṣāl** and **wajd**

MZABITES – Inhabitants of the Mzab in Algeria who adopted the doctrines of **Ibadite Kharijism** in the tenth century.
See **Azraqites**, **Najadāt** and **Ṣufrites**

N

NABĪ, pl. **ANBIYĀ'** – See **prophets** and **qiṣṣa**.

NABĪ (al-) – "The **Prophet**". Name given to **Muḥammad**.
See **nubuwwa**

NABĪDH – Fermented drink, sometimes permitted despite the prohibition of **wine**.

NADAMA – "Regret, repentance".
See **tawba** and **yawm al-ḥasara**

NADHĪR (al-) – "The Warner". Name given to **Muḥammad**.

NADHR – "Vow, votive gift". Particularly in expressions of popular devotion, for example after the birth of a child.

NAFAQA – In legal language, "expense". Expression used in treatises on religious law (**fiqh**) with reference to a husband's duty to provide for his **wife**.

See **marriage** and **women**

NAFAR – "Flight or race" of the pilgrims at certain ritual times during the period of the **ḥajj**.

See **ifāḍa**

NAFS – "Human being" and sometimes "soul" or "passion". – Some theologians maintain that humans are made up of a body and spiritual substance called *nafs*. The **falāsifa**, on the other hand, follow the Aristotelian view that differentiates between the human soul, the animal soul and the vegetable soul. – Mystical writers like al-Ghazāli (died 1111) distinguish between three types of soul, the lower soul, seat of the passions and also called "the soul that commands evil", (*al-nafs al-ammāra bi-l-su'*), "the soul that reproaches" (*al-nafs al-lawwāma*), and the "soothed" or "peaceful" soul, the **mutma'inna**. – The **Ismā'īlī Shī'ites** believe in a universal Soul engendered by the Intellect (**'aql**) from which the world emanates.

See **qalb** and **rūḥ**

NAJADĀT – One of the branches of **Khārijism** that spread in Arabia in the seventh century.

See **Azraqites**, **Ibāḍites**, **Mzabites** and **Ṣufrites**.

NAJAF – Town in Iraq near Kufa that grew up around the **mausoleum** of **'Alī**, murdered in 661 by a **Kharijite** called Ibn Muljam. One of the holy towns of **Shī'ism**.

NAJRĀN – Place in Arabia occupied in the early years of Islam by **Christians** who refused **Muḥammad's** offer of trial by ordeal (**mubāhala**). They were granted freedom of worship in exchange for a proportion of their production. – This agreement inspired the treaties of capitulation signed later in the period of the great **conquests**. It continued in force under the first **caliph Abū Bakr** but the second caliph, **'Umar**, decided to expel the **Jews** and the Christians including those of Najrān, justifying his decision with a tradition (**ḥadīth**) attributed to Muḥammad saying that there should be only one religion in Arabia.

See **dār al-ṣulḥ**, **dhimmī** and **Khaybar**

NAMĀZ – Name given to the ritual prayer (**ṣalāt**) in Iran and Turkey.

NAMĀZGĀH – Persian equivalent of the Arabic **muṣallā**.

NAQD – In the language of religious law (**fiqh**), "part of the dowry payable in cash" at the moment of a **marriage**.

See **mahr** and **ṣadāq**

NAQĪB – "Representative, political administrator". Term used at the time of the **Abbasid** revolution in the eighth century. – The position continued under the **Ismā'īlī Shī'ite** dynasty of the **Fāṭimids** (tenth to twelfth centuries) but disappeared under the 'Abbāsid **caliphs** except in the expression *naqīb al-ashrāf* meaning the "representative of the **sharīfs**" or **Hāshimids**.

NAQL – "Transmitted text". – Used of those pieces of evidence relying on traditional transmission, meaning the **Qur'ān** and the **ḥadīth**, as opposed to those relying on "reason" (**'aql**).

NAQLĪ – "Based on tradition".

See **'ulūm al-naqliyya (al-)**

NAQSHABANDIYYA – **Sūfī brotherhood** founded by al-Naqshabandī (died 1389) that spread particularly in Anatolia and Central Asia.

NĀR – "Fire". Term generally used to refer to **hell** in the **Qur'ān**.

See **damned**, **jahannam**, **sa'īr** and **yawm al-dīn**

NASAB – "Filiation" or part of a **personal name** indicating the sometimes long series of names of a person's father and ancestors, each preceded by the term **ibn** or *ben*, meaning "son of". One of the elements of this list was sometimes retained as a person's main name. – Kinship is based in law on **marriage**. In cases where there is doubt, the husband is considered to be the father, according to the principle of *al-walad li-l-firāsh*, "the child belongs to the bed". The father can object, using the "oath of anathema" (**li'ān**).

NASĀ'Ī (al-) – Author (died 915), working in Damascus, of one of the six canonical collections of traditions (**ḥadīth**).

NAṢĀRĀ – "Christians". Criticised in the **Qur'ān**. After the **conquests** they were granted the status of protected tributaries (**dhimmīs**).

See **ahl al-kitāb**, **monotheism** and **Najrān**

NĀSIKH – "Abrogating". Term used of verses (**āyāt**) in the **Qur'ān**.

See **abrogation**

NAṢṢ – Lit. "text". Term used by **Shī'ites** of the "testamentary designation" that legitimates the authority of a new **imām** on his succession. – This principle, as applied to the devolution of the **imamate**, or, in other words, of power over the Muslim **community**, contrasts with that of "choice" (**ikhtiyār**) adopted by the **Sunnīs**.

NĀṬIQ (al-) – The "speaker". Name given by the **Ismā'īlī Shī'ites** to the interpreter of the "hidden" **imām**.

See **ṣāmit**

NATURAL DISPOSITION – Philosophical term.

See **fiṭra**

NAWĀFIL – In the language of religious law (**fiqh**), "supplementary ritual prayers". – These may be performed after one of the five obligatory daily prayers (**ṣalāt**).

NAZALA – "To come down". – Verb used metaphorically in the **Qur'ān** of God's **revelation**. From it are derived two further words of importance in the religious vocabulary, **nuzūl** and **tanzīl**.

NECESSITY – Used in a legal context.

See **ḍarūra**

NEO- ISMĀ'ĪLIS – See **Nizārīs**.

NIGHT JOURNEY of MUḤAMMAD – Mentioned in the **Qur'ān**.

See **isrā'**

NIKĀḤ – See **marriage**.

NISĀ' – See **women**.

NISBA – Element in a **personal name** indicating one of the following: birthplace of a person or his family, place of residence, vocation, **tribe** or **school of law** to which he belongs. Several nisbas can be used together in order to distinguish one person from another.

NIYYA – In the language of religious law (**fiqh**), "intention". – Fundamental idea in daily life because, according to the Tradition (**ḥadīth**), actions only have validity through the intention behind them.

NIZĀRĪS or **NIZĀRIYYA** – Members of a politico-religious **movement** that brought together those **Sevener Ismā'īlī Shī'ites** who followed the eldest son of the **Fāṭimid caliph** al-Mustanṣir, known as Nizār, whose claims to power were recognised only by them. – Also known as Neo-Ismā'īlīs, they rose up in 1094 under the leadership of Ḥasan-i Ṣabbāḥ, basing themselves mainly around the castle of Alamut in Iran, making sorties to attack the Seljuq **sultans**, the Abbasid caliphs and high-ranking officials of the Seljuq government. – A number of Nizārīs established themselves in fortresses in Syria from which they organised political murders in the twelfth century that earned them the name of **Assassins**. Their leader was Rashīd al-Dīn Sinān, called the "Old Man of the Mountain" by the Franks. – The Nizārīs had their own doctrine. In 1164, they proclaimed the "resurrection" (**qiyāma**) which led to the abolishing of the traditional religious law (**Sharī'a**). Although their states fell, they survived. In the nineteenth century, a new **imām** appeared to lead their diaspora under the title of the **Aga Khan**.

See **hodjas**

NOBLES – "Figures of illustrious descent" such as "members of the great Arab families" and hence "descendants of **Muḥammad**" for whom the terms used are **sharīf** and **sayyid**. – In a more general sense, "people of quality" (*khāṣṣa*) as opposed to *'āmma*, the "crowd" or "plebeians". The word **a'yān** ("notables") is also used.

NUBUWWA – Quality of **prophet** (**nabi**). – Term found in theological discussions where it is used in reference to those sections of works of **kalām** dealing with matters concerning prophesy.

NŪḤ – Noah. Biblical figure mentioned several times in the **Qur'ān**

where one of the **sūras** bears his name. He is presented as a **prophet** whose warnings were ignored by his people who were punished by the Flood. – Later commentaries establish locations for some of the episodes recounted in the Qur'ān, and the **tomb** of Noah is venerated both in **Hebron** and at a site in Lebanon.

NŪR – "Light". Mentioned several times in the **Qur'ān** as being a manifestation of God: "God is the light of the heavens and the earth". The **falāsifa** later produced a Neo-Platonic interpretation. – A long verse evokes this light as a lamp (*miṣbāḥ*), fed by the pure oil of a sacred olive tree, burning in a niche (*mishkāt*). The image of a lamp hanging within an arch evoking a **miḥrāb** is one of the few realistic motifs found in Islamic decorative art. – An emphasis on light becomes apparent from the Middle Ages when the **mosques** and sanctuaries began to be decorated with lamps and other forms of **lighting**.

NUSAYRĪS – Also called Alawites or "followers of **'Alī**". Extremist **Shī'ites** (**ghulāt**) belonging to a politico-religious **movement** that broke away from **Twelver Imāmism** in the ninth century. – The founder of the movement had supported the Tenth **'Alid Imām**, **'Ali al-Hādī**, setting himself up as spokesman (**bāb**) for this imām whom he claimed was an incarnation of God. The doctrine of the movement, which included secret rituals and initiation rites, incorporated elements of Christianity and Zoroastrianism. – A community that had settled in ancient times in an area of Syria was recognised in 1922 by the French government as an Alawite State. This did not survive the end of the French Mandate in the late 1930s. – Today, Alawites play an important role in Syrian political life.

See **firqa**

NUZŪL – Lit. "descent". Following one of the meanings of **nazala**, "manner of **revelation** of the **Qur'ān**".

See **asbāb al-nuzūl** and **tanzīl**

O

OATH – The "judicial oath" (*yamīn*) can have a legal value in certain circumstances, particularly when taken before a **qāḍī**. – Other special oaths exist including the "oath of allegiance" (**bay'a**), also called the "oath of fidelity", and the "oath of anathema" (**li'ān**).

OBEDIENCE – Term used in legal language. See **tā'ab** and **ulu'l-amr**.

OBLIGATORY – Legal adjective used of **human actions**.
See **wājib**

OCCULTATION – Period of absence of the **Imām** as believed by some **Shī'ites**.
See **ghayba**

OFFER – Legal term used in contracts.
See **ījāb**

OMNIPOTENT (the) – One of the **Beautiful Names of God**.
See **Qādir (al-)**

ONENESS of GOD – See **tawḥīd**.

OPPRESSED – **Qur'ānic** term.
See **mustaḍ 'afūn**

ORATORY – See **masjid**.

ORGANISER (the) – One of the **Beautiful Names of God**.
See **Muṣawwir (al-)**

ORPHAN – Mentioned in the **Qur'ān**.
See **yatīm**

ORTHODOXY – The doctrine of the first Muslims (**salaf**). – Since schisms emerged very early on as a result of the various and often opposing politico-religious **movements**, orthodoxy has to be defined as that doctrine professed by the greatest number, in other words, the **Sunnīs** (**ahl al-Sunna wa'l-jāmā'a**).

P

PACT – See **'ahd**, **mīthāq** and **ṣaḥīfa**.

PALACE – Arabic *qaṣr*, pl. *quṣūr* and sometimes *dār*. – In the period of the **caliphate**, palaces fulfilled the need for a place for ceremonial occasions imitated from ancient usage. These were markedly different from the simplicity of the first gatherings of the **community** in the Great Mosque (**jāmi'**). Their function was to express the power and pomp of the defender of Islam, while at the same time respecting the simplicity of a dwelling place with its characteristic architectural elements dictated by the custom of polygamy and the need to confine **women** to the **harem**. – The palace served as a model for the residences of other dignitaries and, in the provinces, of the homes of **governors** called in former times **dār al-imāra** ("The dwelling of command"). – Later, such palaces were at times replaced by the *ḥisn* or *qal'a*, a fortress or fortified castle behind whose walls local dynasties and other military leaders could feel more secure.

PALANQUIN – See **Camel** (**Battle of the**) and **maḥmal**.

PARADISE – Reserved for the **elect** and described in the **eschatological** sections of the **Qur'ān** as being a garden (**janna**) of delights, populated by **houris** (*ḥūr*). – The "vision of God" (**ru'yat Allāh**) is a matter discussed by the theologians (**mutakallimūn**).

See **firdaws**, **muqarrabūn**, **muttaqūn**, **salām**, **shahīd** and **ṣirāṭ**

PARTY of GOD – See **ḥizb Allāh**.

PATIENCE – Mentioned in the **Qur'ān**.

See **ṣabr**

PATIENCE – **Qur'ānic** concept.

See **ṣabr**

PEACE – See **salām** and **ṣulḥ**.

PEN – Arabic *qalam*. The calamus or reed pen was used by a copyist or secretary, called **kātib**. Mentioned in the opening of one of the **sūras**, the pen appears in the **Qur'ān** as a tool of divine power.

PEOPLE of the BENCH, PEOPLE of the HOUSE, PEOPLE of the BOOK, PEOPLE of the MANTLE, PEOPLE of the PORTICO – See **ahl al-bayt**, **ahl al-kisā'**, **ahl al-kitāb** and **ahl al-ṣuffa**.

PERFUMES – The use of perfumes is **recommended** in certain circumstances, such as during the **pilgrimage**.

PERSONAL NAMES – In early Muslim society, these were made up of a complex collection of several names attached to the name (**ism**) given to a child at **birth**, followed by the "filiation" (**nasab**) and preceded by the **kunya**. – Some birth names are specifically Muslim, such as Muḥammad, Aḥmad, Muṣṭafā which all have the meaning of "worthy of praise" or include the name of God, such as **'Abd Allāh** and **'Abd al-Raḥmān**. Other names are Arab names, such as Mu'āwiya, or come from the familiar stories from the cultures of other Muslim countries, Persian, Turkish or Berber. – To the cluster of names formed by the **kunya**, **ism** and **nisba** are added other appellations, sometimes several. – Of this long list of names, only a few would commonly be used for any given person. There were occasions, however, when all names would be required. Nowadays, the system of personal names has been simplified, often rather arbitrarily, so that each person has a first or given name followed by what is considered to be a family name or surname.

PERSONAL OPINION – Legal term.

See **ra'y**

PETITION – Used to make a complaint about "abuses" (**maẓālim**).

See **ruq'a**

PIETY – Arabic *birr*. Explicitly mentioned in a verse of the **Qur'ān** that states that the pious person should: believe in God, in the Day of Judgement (**yawm al-dīn**), in the Qur'ān and in the **prophets**; be generous to his close relatives (**dhāwu'l-qurba**), to orphans (**yatāma**), to the poor (**masākīn**), to a traveller (**ibn al-sabīl**) and to beggars (**sā'ilūn**); perform the ritual prayer (**ṣalāt**) and pay the obligatory alms (**zakāt**). In addition, forms of popular piety exist involving non-canonical devotions (personal supplication, the cult of the **saints**) and various traditions that sometimes have elements of **magic**, all of which seek to invoke God's **help**.

See **arkān al-dīn**, **'ibādāt** and **taqwā**

PILGRIMAGE – Term used of several different practices. – The most important is the major pilgrimage to **Mecca** (**ḥajj**), mentioned in the **Qur'ān** and one of the five pillars of Islam (**arkān al-dīn**). Obligatory for most Muslims, it takes place every year on the same date in the month of **dhu'l-ḥijja**. It was observed by **Muḥammad** who integrated a number of pre-Islamic elements into the ritual. – The minor pilgrimage (**'umra**) is additional and takes place at Mecca around the **Ka'ba**. It can be performed as often as desired, at any time of year, and will earn the pilgrim merit. It may be carried out in conjunction with the **ḥajj**. – The "secondary pilgrimages" (**ziyāras**), better defined as "pious visits", are made to venerated objects found in all parts of the Islamic world. The non-canonical rituals associated with these places are sometimes called the "cult of **saints**".

PILLARS of ISLAM – See **arkān al-dīn**.

PILLARS of STONES of MINĀ (**the three**) – See **jamarāt**.

PIOUS – See **muqarrabūn**, **muttaqūn** and **sāliḥūn**.

PIOUS VISIT – "Secondary pilgrimage".

See **mazār** and **ziyāra**

PĪR – In Persia, a person respected for his age and experience of **mysticism**. Hence the "spiritual guide, master" of a **Ṣūfī fraternity**.

See **shaykh**

PLEDGE – Legal term.

See **rahn**

POLE – In connection with sanctity.

See **quṭb**

POLICE (chief of) – See **ṣāḥib al-shurṭa**.

POLICY or POLITICS – Consistent with the religious law.
See **siyāsa shar'iyya**

POLYGAMY – See **marriage**.

PORK – The eating of this meat is forbidden by the **Qur'ān**.
See **dietary laws**

PORTICO – See **ahl al-suffa** and **riwāq**.

POSSESSORS of the SCRIPTURE – Expression used in the **Qur'ān**.
See **ahl al-kitāb**

POVERTY – There are two words for poverty: *faqr*, the voluntary poverty of **Muḥammad** recommended by **Ṣūfīs** and emulated by an ascetic (**zāhid**) who has no personal possessions; **maskīn**, the poverty of those to whom the **Qur'ān** says alms should be given.
See **dervish**, **faqīr** and **piety**

POWERFUL (the) – One of the names used of God.
See **'Azīz (al-)**

PREACHER – Official, mystical or popular.
See **khatīb**, **qāṣṣ** and **wā'iẓ**

PRAISE, PRAISE to GOD – See **doxologies**, **al-ḥamdu li-llāh**, **madḥ** and **manāqib**.

PRAYER – Prayer falls into two categories: – ritual prayer (**ṣalāt**), used of the obligatory daily prayers, supplementary prayer (**nawāfil**) and the solemn Friday prayers; – personal and individual supplications called **du'ā'** or **kunūt** to which can be added certain litanies, **dhikr** and **wird**, recited mainly by **Ṣūfīs**.

PREDECESSORS – See **sābiqūn**.

PREDESTINATION – Arabic **qaḍā'**. Accepted, sometimes with reservations, by the majority of **schools of theology**. – The **Mu'tazilites** who see God's decree (**qadar**) as being limited are the only group to assert the existence of **free will**.
See **Jabrites**, **Murjites** and **Qadarites**

PROCLAMATION of FAITH – See **shahāda**.

PROFESSION of FAITH – See **'aqīda** and **shahāda**.
PROOF – See **bayyina**, **burhān**, **dalīl**, **ḥujja** and **ḥujjat al-islām**.
PROPAGANDA – Political and religious.
See **da'wa**
PROPERTY and MORTMAIN – See **milk** and **waqf**.
PROPHETS – Arabic *nabī* pl. *anbiyā'*. "Those sent by God to deliver a message to humankind" warning them of God's punishment (**'adhāb**). **Muḥammad**, the "seal of the prophets" (**khatam al-anbiyā'**), is of their number. – Many of the prophets mentioned in the **Qur'ān** are known from the Bible where they are only rarely referred to as prophets: **Adam** and his family, **Nūḥ**/Noah, **Ibrāhīm**/Abraham, **Lūṭ**/Lot, **Isḥāq**/Isaac, **Ismā'īl**/Ismael, **Ya'qūb**/Jacob, **Yūsuf**/Joseph, **Mūsā**/Moses, **Shu'ayb**/Jethro, **Hārūn**/Aaron, **Dāwūd**/David, **Sulaymān**/Solomon, **Ilyās**/Elijah, **al-Yasa'**/Elisha, **Dhu'l Kifl**/Ezekiel, **Ayyūb**/Job, **Yūnus**/Jonah, **Zakarīyā'**/ Zachariah, **Yaḥyā**/John and **'Īsā**/Jesus. – To these can be added those believed to have been sent to ancient Arab tribes, including Muḥammad's immediate predecessors **Hūd** and **Ṣāliḥ**.
See **nubuwwa** and **qiṣṣa**
PROPRIETY – A frequently invoked idea in Muslim society and daily life. – The rules of correct behaviour are enumerated in the treatises on religious law (**fiqh**) and in the collections of **ḥadīth**. They concern subjects such as clothing, the wearing of jewellery, the correct styles of greeting, and they incorporate and Islamicise the traditional Persian **adab**.
See **kunya** and **veil**
PROSTRATION – During ritual prayer (**ṣalāt**).
See **sujūd**
PROVINCES – Of the **Dār al-Islām**.
See **emir**, **governors**, **wāli** and **wilāya**
PUBLIC FOUNTAINS – Arabic **sabīl**. Numerous examples can be found, sometimes alone, sometimes as part of an architectural complexes such as a **madrasa** or **kuttāb**, constructed as pious foundations and financed by the system of "mortmain"

(**waqfs**) allowing property to be endowed in perpetuity.

PUNISHMENTS, LEGAL and DISCRETIONARY – See **ḥadd** and **ta‘zīr**.

PURDAH – "Seclusion". Term used in India to describe the situation of **women** who are obliged to stay at home or, if going out, cover themselves with a **veil**.

See **harem**

PURE (**the**) – **Qur'ānic** expression.

See **abrār**

Q

QĀBIL – Cain. Biblical figure mentioned in the **Qur'ān**.

QABR – See **'adhāb al-qabr**, **mausoleum**, **death** and **tomb**.

QABŪL – "Acceptance". Legal term appearing in contracts of **sale** to indicate the purchaser's agreement. Corresponds to the receiving of the object.

See **ījāb** and **selling**

QAḌĀ' – "Decision or sentence"; from which is derived the sense of "function of a **qāḍī**". – In theological language it can also mean **predestination**.

QADAM – "Footprint" of a **prophet** or **saint** appearing on certain venerated stones. – The print of **Ibrāhīm**/Abraham's foot is found on the stone known as Ibrāhīm's **maqām** venerated near the **Ka'ba**. – Other stones or rocks are also held to be sacred in many parts of the Muslim world. **Mosques** in India have been built to house the footprints of **Muḥammad** *qadam-i rasūl* in stones brought back from Arabia by pilgrims.

QADAR – "Divine decree".

See **Jabrites**, **free will**, **Murjites** and **Qadarites**

QADARITES – Name given to those who believe that the importance of the divine decree (**qadar**) is limited, maintaining that humans have **free will** and are responsible for their actions.

See **Jabrites**, **Murjites** and **Mu'tazilites**

QADHF – In legal language, “false accusation of fornication” (**zinā’**).

QĀḌĪ – “Judge”. Arabic *qāḍī*, pl. *quḍāt*. – In the Muslim territories of the **Dār al-Islām**, he was the agent of the ruler entrusted with the task of overseeing “civil and criminal jurisdiction” (**qaḍā’**) in the name of religious law (**fiqh**). This meant that he was able to impose orders on the community in line with the demands of religious law (**Sharī‘a**). – During the Middle Ages a qāḍī had to hand out judgement in the case of private disputes, applied the rules relating to **civil status** such as those concerning **marriage** and **inheritance** and impose legal penalties (**ḥadd**), his decisions being carried out by the chief of police (**ṣāḥib al-shurṭa**). – In uncertain cases, he could call upon one or several jurists (**faqīh**) for or an opinion (**fatwā**) which he would follow or not as he saw fit. – He was assisted by “professional witnesses” (**‘ādil**, pl. **‘udūl**). – The office of **supreme chief qāḍī** emerged in the eighth century.

See **maḥkama**

QĀDIR (al-) – “The All-Powerful”. One of the **Beautiful Names of God**.

QĀDIRIYYA – **Ṣūfī fraternity** founded in the twelfth century by ‘Abd al-Qādir al-Jilānī (died 1165) that flourished in Iraq, Syria, Anatolia, India and Africa.

QĀHIRA (al-) – “The Victorious”. Arabic name for the city of **Cairo**.

QĀ’IDA, pl. **QAWĀ’ID** – In a religious context, “rule, established principle”.

QALAM – See **pen**.

QALANDARIYYA – **Ṣūfī fraternity** founded in the thirteenth century in Khurāsān and expanding into India. The members were characterised by their unusual customs and bizarre ascetic practices.

QALANSUWWA – Part of male headwear worn by important figures in the Middle Ages, particularly the **caliph**, under a turban (**‘imāma**).

QALB – "Heart". Organ associated in the **Qur'ān** with the knowledge of God. – Organ associated with conscience and foundation of personality for the **mystic** writers who considered **Ṣūfism** to be the "science of hearts" (**'ilm al-qulūb**).

See **'aql**, **nafs**, **rūḥ** and **ta'līf al-qulūb**

QĀNŪN – Term originating from Greek. – "Administrative regulation" that, during Ottoman rule, specified the application of a particular disposition of the law (**Sharī'a**) and sometimes modified it with the introduction of a secular law decreed by the **sultan**. It applied chiefly to penal law and taxation.

QARA'A – "Read, recite". Verb giving the root for several words in the religious vocabulary including **Qur'ān**.

See **iqra'**, **qāri'** and **qirā'a**

QĀRI', pl. **QURRĀ'** – "Reader" of the **Qur'ān** versed in the method and established rules of recitation, – either a professional reader, employed to read the Qur'ān in, for example, a mausoleum, or a pious man who has devoted himself to the study and recitation of the holy text. – The plural form of the word usually refers to the seven "readers" who laid down the authorised variants or **readings** accepted by the **Sunnīs**.

QARĪ'A (al-) – Lit. "That which shatters", sometimes translated as "disaster" or "repelling calamity". Title of an early **sūra** in the **Qur'ān** announcing the end of the world.

See **yawm al-dīn**

QARMAṬĪ – Arabic *al-Qarāmita*. Followers of a politico-religious **movement** derived from **Shī'ite Ismā'īlism** founded by Hamdān Qarmat in the Kufa area and which recognised **Muḥammad ibn Ismā'īl** as Seventh **Imām**. – They rose up in 899 against the Ismā'īlī authorities of Salamiyya in Syria, the last leader of the rebels being captured by the '**Abbāsid** army and executed in Baghdad in 904. Other insurgents attempted to win over Kufa but were defeated in 907. Another group, who had settled in Baḥrayn in 886, had attacked Baṣra and the **ḥajj** caravans, going so far as to capture the **Black Stone**, removing it from the **Ka'ba** in 929 (to which it was restored in 951). – The movement came to an end in the eleventh century after opposition from the **Fāṭimids**.

QAṢR, pl. **QUṢŪR** – See **palace**.

QĀṢṢ, pl. **QUṢṢĀS** – "Popular preacher" who would sit by the roadside to relate edifying stories (*qaṣaṣ*) of a theological and political nature. As a result, it was an activity often made use of by the authorities.

See **wā'iẓ**

QAṬ' al-ṬARĪQ – Punished by a legal sentence (**ḥadd**).

See **brigandage**

QAYSARIYYA – "Building where precious merchandise is traded", regulated particularly by the **muḥtasib**. – The term, of ancient origin, was replaced in the East by **khān** and, in North Africa, by ***funduq***, often translated as "caravanserai" although with a wider meaning.

See **bazār**, **ḥisba** and **market**

QAYYIM al-KITĀB – "The keeper of the Book". One of the titles given by **Shī'ītes** to their **imām**.

QAYYŪM (al) – "The enduring". One of the **Beautiful Names of God**.

QIBLA – Direction of **Mecca** towards which the faithful should turn to perform the ritual prayer (**ṣalāt**). Every **mosque** (**masjid**) is oriented by its back wall (***qibla***) in which the niche of the **miḥrāb** is placed. – **Muḥammad** originally chose the direction of **Jerusalem** but, after the Battle of the Ditch (**Khandaq**) and the execution of the **Jews** of the Qurayẓa tribe, he adopted the new and definitive direction, as stated in a verse in the **Qur'ān**.

See **abrogation**

QIMĀR – "Gambling". Forbidden by the **Qur'ān**.

QIRĀ'A, pl. **QIRA'ĀT** – See **Readings of the Qur'ān**.

QIRĀḌ – In legal language, "share, association of capital and work for a commercial undertaking". Such an arrangement makes it possible to lend money and receive part of the ensuing profit without "lending with interest" (**ribā**) which is forbidden in Islam.

QIRĀN – Particular way of performing the **Pilgrimage** to **Mecca**, when the **'umra** and the **ḥajj** are completed together.
See **tamattu'**

QIṢĀṢ – In the language of religious law (**fiqh**), "retaliation". – Ancient practice in Arabia accepted with some modifications by the **Qur'ān**, according to which, for example, the representative of the victim has the right to vengeance (**tha'r**) as long as it is not extreme. Alternatively, the guilty party may be pardoned if blood money (**diya**) is paid.

QIṢṢA, pl. **QIṢAṢ** – "Story, account". – The *qiṣaṣ al-anbiyā'* ("stories of the history of the **prophets**") told in specific works bearing this name are drawn both from the **Qur'ān** and from other later traditions of various origins.

QIYĀMA – According to the **Qur'ān**, the "resurrection of the dead" on the Day of Judgement (**yawm al-dīn**). – For the **Shī'ites** it has the meaning of "spiritual resurrection" that they interpret as the return of the long-awaited last **imām**. The ***qiyāma*** was proclaimed by the **Nizārīs** in 1164.
See **resurrection of the dead**

QIYĀS – "Reasoning by analogy". – Used by jurists (**faqīhs**) to resolve problems of religious law (**fiqh**) not clarified in the texts. – It was first developed by al-Shāfi'ī (died 820) on the basis of his study of the effective cause (**'illa**) of a decision that might lead to other unforeseen decisions and used subsequently in the **Shāfi'ī** school of law. – Later al-Ghazālī (died 1111) sought to justify the logical nature of such reasoning.

QUBBA – "Cupola". – Also used of a whole building in the case of **mausoleums** and small sanctuaries (**mazars**) commemorating a **saint** and containing some venerated object. – In North Africa such buildings are also known as **marabouts**.
See **murābiṭ**

QUBBAT al-SAKHRA – See **Dome of the Rock**.

QUDDŪS (al-) – "The Holy". One of the **Beautiful Names of God**.

QUDS (al-) – Present-day Arabic name for **Jerusalem**. Formed from a root meaning "sanctity".

QUDSĪ – "Holy, sacred". – Adjective used of a tradition (**ḥadīth**) believed to be the word of God transmitted to **Muḥammad** by inspiration.

QUL – In Turkish, **slave**. Used more specifically of the slaves belonging to the Ottoman **sultans**.

QUM – Or Qom – Holy city for the **Imāmī Shī'ites** of Iran where the sister of the Eighth **Imām 'Alī al-Riḍā** is buried. Her **tomb** is the object of pious visits (**ziyāras**) and is surrounded by many religious foundations and **madāris** where future **mullahs** receive instruction.

QUR'ĀN – Arabic **qur'ān**, meaning "recitation", referring to the entirety of the message transmitted by **Muḥammad** and collected together by his **Companions**. – The verb **qara'a**, "to recite", appears several times in the Qur'ān, particularly in the imperative form **iqrā'** in the line: "Recite, in the name of the Lord who created". It is twice accompanied by the adjective **Arabic**, thus emphasising that this is the language chosen for God's **revelation**. – The Qur'ān consists of 114 **sūras** (chapters), each of between 3 and 287 verses (**āyāt**). Tradition says that it was written down after the death of Muḥammad by his secretary **Zayd ibn Thābit**. Then, still according to tradition, the **caliph 'Uthmān** established an official version of which several copies were made and distributed from **Medina** to the cities of Basra, Kufa and **Damascus**. – The sūras of the Qur'ān are arranged according to length, the longest, with the exception of the **fātiḥa**, coming first. Traditionally attributed to either the **Mecca** or the **Medina** period, each sūra is considered as a single entity. Using internal textual evidence, scholars have attempted to establish a more precise chronology of the various fragments that they have identified. – Other divisions of the text, **ḥizb** and **juz'**, have come about for solely practical reasons related to recitation.

See **abrogation**, **i'jāz**, **muḥkam** and **mutashabbih**

QUR'ĀNIC VERSES – See **āyāt**.

QURAYSH – **Arab tribe** from **Mecca** to which **Muḥammad** belonged. – It consisted of two important clans, the **Hashimites**, Muḥammad's clan, and the more powerful 'Abd Shams clan. – The **Umayyads** who took power in 660 were of the 'Abd Shams clan while the **'Abbāsids** who came to power in 750 were descended from **al-'Abbās**, Muḥammad's uncle. – **Sunnī** jurists (**faqīhs**) established a rule that the **caliphate** could only be occupied by a descendant of the Quraysh tribe.

QURRĀ' – pl. of **qāri'** or "readers of the **Qur'ān**".

QUṬB – "Pole". – Name given to the **saint** who, according to certain **Ṣūfī** doctrines, stands at the head of a hierarchy of **apotropaic saints** called **abdāl** and **abrār**. This "pole" is believed to support the world.

See **ghawth**

R

RABB – "Master, lord" when speaking of God for whom this term, frequently used in the **Qur'ān**, is reserved.

See **rubūbiyya**

RABB al-'ĀLAMĪN – "Master or lord of the worlds".

See **'ālam**

RABĪ 'I and II – Third and fourth **lunar months** of the Islamic **calendar**. – The birth and death of **Muḥammad** are commemorated during Rabī' I with the festival of the **mawlid**. – In Rabī' II, the members of the **fraternity** of the **Qādiriyya** in India hold a festival commemorating their founder 'Abd al-Qādir al-Gīlānī.

RAHBĀNIYYA – See **monasticism**.

RAḤĪM (al-) – "The Merciful". One of the **Beautiful Names of God**. Made popular through the **basmala**.

See **raḥma**

RAḤMA – "Clemency, mercy, benevolence". One of the central qualities of God according to the **Qur'ān**. Whence the titles of **Raḥmān** and **Raḥīm**.

RAḤMA (jabal al-) – "Mountain of Mercy", dominating the plain of **'Arafāt** where the "station" (**wuqūf**) is performed during the **ḥajj**. A path up the mound was constructed during the Middle Ages, the summit of which is crowned by a small sanctuary (**qubba**) alongside which, in the twelfth century, the **caliph's standards** were placed at the time of the **ḥajj**.

RAḤMĀN (al-) – "The Merciful". One of the **Beautiful Names of God**. Popularised through the **basmala**.

See **'Abd al-Raḥmān** and **raḥma**

RAHN – In legal language, "security", or sum given in pledge.

RAJAB – Seventh **month** of the Islamic **calendar**, often called *fard*, "isolated". The month in which **Muḥammad**'s Night Journey (**isrā'**) took place and when it continues to be commemorated.

RAJĪM (al-) – The "stoned one". Or, more accurately, "he who deserves to be stoned", meaning the "cursed one". – This expression from the **Qur'ān** refers to **Iblīs** who is often called **al-Shayṭān** *al-rajīm* or "the cursed Devil".

RAK'A – Sequence forming a unit of the ritual prayer (**ṣalāt**). One *rak'a* consists of: – the recitation of the **Fātiḥa**;– a bow made by placing the hands on the knees; – straightening up; – prostration (**sujūd**); – a second prostration and the recitation of the "proclamation of faith" (**shahāda**) in a kneeling position.

RAMAḌĀN – Ninth month of the Muslim year during which a fast (**ṣawm**) is observed. The month is called "holy". – The "night of destiny" (**laylat al-qadar**) is celebrated during this month which ends with the "minor" festival of **'īd al-ṣaghīr**.

RĀSHIDŪN – The "Rightly Guided". Expression used of the first four **caliphs** of Islam, **Abū Bakr**, **'Umar**, **'Uthmān** and **'Ali**, chosen by election after the death of **Muḥammad** and numbering among his first **Companions**.

RASŪL or **RASŪL ALLĀH** – Name given to **Muḥammad**.

See **messenger**

RATIONALISTS – Term sometimes used in reference to the **Mu'tazilites** who sought to present the elements of their "belief" (**īmān**) as being consistent with "reason" (**'aql**). It was never their belief, however, that the truth could be arrived at through reason: the term "rationalising" would therefore be more accurate.

RAWĀFIḌ – "Those who reject". Pejorative term used by **Sunnīs** of **Shī'ites** who challenge or "reject" the legitimacy of the three first **caliphs** of the **Rashidūn**.

RAWḌA – "Garden". One of the terms used to refer to a **tomb**, particularly one of a **saint**. – Used of two venerated spots in the **mosque** at **Medina**: – the spot where **Muḥammad** stood next to the **minbar**; – the enclosed area around his tomb and those of **Abū Bakr** and **'Umar**, his original **Companions** and later the first two **caliphs**.

RA'Y – "Personal opinion". – Used by certain jurists (**faqīhs**) opposed to the **traditionalists** when interpreting religious law (**fiqh**). – Among the **schools of law**, it was predominantly used by **Hanafites**.

See **ijtihād**

RAYĀT – See **standards**.

READINGS of the QUR'ĀN – The text of the **Qur'ān** as put together under **Caliph 'Uthmān** in c. 650 permitted a number of different "readings" (*qira'āt*) because it lacked both diacritics (which distinguish certain consonants) and vocalic accents. – It was established in the tenth century that the seven "readings" made by seven eighth-century Qur'ānic scholars should be accepted as authoritative. – Today only two versions, that of 'Āsim in Egypt and that of Nāfi' in Africa, are still used while those of Abū 'Amr, Ḥamza, Ibn 'Āmir, Ibn Kathīr and al-Kisā'ī have been set aside. – The **Shī'ites** use a different "reading" that better supports **'Alī**'s claims to power.

See **Ibn Mujāhid** and **qāri'**

REALITY, RELIGIOUS and SPIRITUAL – See **ḥaqq**.

REASON – See **‘aql** and **rationalists**.

REASONING – See **‘aql**, **qiyās**, **‘ulūm al-‘aqliyya** and **uṣūl al-fiqh**.

RECITATION – See **Qur’ān**, **iqra’**, **qara’a**, **qāri’ and qirā’a**.

RECOMMENDED – Adjective used in legal language to categorise **human actions**.

See **ḥukm**, **mandūb** and **ma‘rūf**

REFLECTION – In the context of the **Qur’ān** see **‘aql**. – In a legal context see **fiqh** and **ijtihād**.

REFORMISM – Introduced at the end of the nineteenth century.

See **iṣlāḥ**

RELIGION – See **dīn**, **milla** and **millet**.

RELIGIOUS LAW – See **Sharī’a** and **fiqh**.

RELIGIOUS OBLIGATIONS – See **arkān al-dīn** and **‘ibādāt**.

REPENTANCE – See **tawba**, **nadama** and **yawm al-ḥasara**.

REPREHENSIBLE – Legal term used to categorise **human actions**.

See **ḥukm**, **makrūh** and **munkar**

REPUDIATION – Arabic *ṭalāq*. According to religious law (**fiqh**), this consists of saying three times “I repudiate you”. Such an action cannot be revoked unless in the interim the woman has remarried and divorced another husband. – In cases of repudiation the husband must give the whole of the marriage gift (**ṣadāq**) to his wife.

See **divorce** and **marriage**

RESPONSIBILITY – Of humankind see **free will**. – As legal term see **damān** and **mukallaf**.

RESURRECTION of the DEAD – Arabic **qiyāma**, which can also refer to the “spiritual resurrection” awaited by some **Shī‘ites**. – It will take place, according to the **Qur’ān**, at the end of the world on the Day of Judgement (**yawm al-dīn**). – The **falāsifa** found this notion difficult to accept, whereas, like other eschatological themes, it constitutes a favourite subject of popular literature based in the Tradition (**ḥadīth**).

RETALIATION – Legal term.
See **qiṣāṣ**

REVELATION – Fundamental concept in Islam. – Expressed by the Arabic terms **firqān**, **iqra'**, **nuzūl**, **tanzīl** and **waḥy**. – The **Qur'ān** is considered to be an intangible text, in **Arabic**, dictated by God to **Muḥammad** through the intermediary of the **angel Jibrīl**. This has presented difficulties for certain **exegeses**.
See **"created" Qur'ān**

RIBĀ – "Lending with interest", or sometimes "usury". Condemned in several verses of the **Qur'ān**, one of which specifies: "Believers, do not live on usury, doubling your wealth many times over". –Absolutely forbidden by jurists (**faqīhs**), this did not prevent, in former times, illegal lending or ingenious methods to get round the prohibition by legal means, one of which was the "share" (**qirāḍ**), a form of profit-sharing. – Today it has become possible to set up banks that are able to justify **ribā** by presenting the low levels of interest paid as the remuneration for a service.

RIBĀṬ – Building or particularly "fortress" on the land or sea frontiers of the **dār al-Islām** that in early times housed the **murābiṭūn**, warriors of the **jihād**, who lived there according to the rules of their religion (**'ibādāt**). The **ribāṭs** in Tunisia dating from the ninth-century Aghlabid period are of this type. – Also one of the terms used for a **Ṣūfī monastery**. – In Iran, a "caravanserai" where travellers could stay safely overnight with their merchandise.

RIḌĀ – In the language of the **mystics**, "divine delight". One of the stages through which a **Ṣūfī** must pass on his spiritual journey.
See **'Ali al-Riḍā**, **ḥāl**, **manzil** and **maqāma**

RIDDA – "Apostasy". – Used first of the rebellion of the Arab **tribes** who, after the death of **Muḥammad**, refused to obey the first **caliph Abū Bakr** and who were vigorously opposed. – It later came to mean any departure by a Muslim from the practices or beliefs of Islam. Punishable by death according to a legal sentence (**ḥadd**).

RIḌWĀN (**bay'at al-**) – "Oath of satisfaction". Oath of allegiance (**bay'a**) made by the **Companions** to **Muḥammad**, promising to follow him in all his decisions at the time when he was negotiating a truce at **Hudaybiyya** with the people of **Mecca**. Also called the **bay'at al-shajara**.

RIFĀ'IYYA – **Ṣūfī fraternity** founded in Iraq by Ahmad al-Rifā'ī (died 1182). It spread as far as India but flourished particularly in Anatolia.

RISĀLA – "Epistle, treatise". In the language of theology, "mission of the prophet-legislator" (**rasūl**).

RITES – Term often used in the past of the **schools of law**, since the **'ibādat** ("acts of religious adoration") presented in the first section of treatises on religious law (**fiqh**) deal solely with ritual obligations.

RITUAL PURITY – Or legal purity. Arabic *ṭahāra*. Achieved through the performance of **ablutions**. – These must be carried out in order to perform religious duties such as the ritual prayers (**ṣalāt**).

See **ablutions**, **holiness or purity** (**state of**) and **zakāt**

RIWĀQ – "Portico" found in the majority of **mosques** along the sides of the courtyard (**ṣaḥn**) leading to the prayer hall.

RIWĀYA – "Written transmission" of a tradition (**ḥadīth**) or of a work on the **religious sciences**.

RIYĀ' – "Hypocrisy", ostentation in religion.

See **munāfiq**

ROCK – Arabic *sakhra*.

See **Dome of the Rock**

RUBŪBIYYA – "Lordly power of God". Term formed from the word **rabb** that is used frequently in the **Qur'ān**.

RŪḤ – "Spirit". Used in the **Qur'ān** with various meanings including that of the "divine spirit" that appears to **Maryam** in the story of the annunciation. – Refers more generally to "the soul or essence of a thing". – When applied to humans it is the equivalent of **nafs** ("soul"), **qalb** ("heart") or even **'aql**

(“intellect”). It also refers to the vital principle or breath.

RUQ‘A – “Petition” or request that a Muslim can present to a sovereign or his representative when seeking redress for an “abuse”.

See **dār al-‘adl** and **maẓālim**

RU’YAT ALLĀH – “Sight of God” in **Paradise**. – Considered as possible by the majority of **mutakallimūn** but as impossible by the **Mu‘tazilites**.

S

SĀ‘A – According to the **Qur’ān**, the “Hour” that none can escape, the Day of Judgement (**yawm al-dīn**).

SABAB, pl. **ASBĀB** – In theological language, “motive, cause”.

See **Asbāb al-nuzūl**

SABB – “Insult”. – The punishment for insulting **Muḥammad** is death, both for Muslims and also for **dhimmīs**.

SABĪL – In religious and literary language, “way, path”. The formula *fī sabīl Allāh* meaning “in the path of God” appears in the **Qur’ān** as does the expression *ibn al-sabīl* (“son of the path”) meaning a “traveller”. – Came to be used also of **public fountains** constructed by pious donors in Muslim towns for the benefit of the poor and travellers.

SĀBIQŪN – The “predecessors”. Mentioned in the **Qur’ān** as standing next to God among the **elect**. – According to some commentators, the expression refers to the first Muslims, meaning those who prayed in the two directions of **Jerusalem** and **Mecca** and who emigrated after the **hijra** and took part in the Battle of **Badr**.

ṢABR – “Constance, patience”. – Recommended by the **Qur’ān** and also by **Ṣūfīs**. One of the characteristics of a devout Muslim.

SACRIFICE (**Day of**) – Tenth day of **dhu’l-ḥijja** when **ḥajj** pilgrims go to the valley of **Minā** to perform a sacrifice commemorating the sacrifice of **Ibrāhīm**/Abraham. On the same day, all over the Muslim world, the same sacrifice is celebrated with **'īd al-kabīr**, the "Major Festival".

See **dhabb**, **dhabīha** and **manhar**

ṢADĀQ – "Dowry" or more accurately "marriage gift" that a husband must pay to his wife at the time when a contract of **marriage** is made. Generally he only pays half of the amount, the other half being paid at a later date according to arrangements specified in the contract. – In the case of **repudiation**, the whole amount passes to the woman.

See **mahr** and **naqd**

ṢADAQA – "Charity, alms". Term referring either to the obligatory alms (**zakāt**), prescribed by the **Qur'ān**, or to an individual act of charity.

ṢAFĀ (**al-**) – Elevated spot near the **Ka'ba** in **Mecca** from which pilgrims must go to a nearby hillock called **al-Marwa** and return, repeating this distance several times to accomplish the ritual of the "race" (**sa'ī**).

ṢAFAR – Second **lunar month** of the Islamic **calendar**. Often called "good" (***khayr***).

ṢAḤĀBA – Pl. of **ṣāḥib**, with the sense of the **Companions of Muḥammad**.

ṢĀḤIB, pl. **AṢḤĀB** – Term with various meanings: "Companion, master, author or possessor". It occurs in various expressions such as **ṣāḥib al-ḥūt**, **ṣāḥib al-shurṭa** and **ṣāḥib al-zamān**. – The plural *aṣḥāb* appears in the **Qur'ān** in various names for the **damned** and the **elect**, referring to their punishment or reward: **aṣḥāb al-janna**, **al-mash'ama**, **al-maymana** and **al-nār**.

ṢĀḤIB al-ḤŪT – "The man with the fish".

See **Yūnus**

ṢĀḤIB al-SHURṬA – "Chief of police". It is his task to ensure the maintenance of law and order in the **dār al-islām** on behalf of the sovereign and to carry out legal sentences (**ḥadd**) imposed by a **qāḍī** on wrongdoers.

ṢĀḤIB al-ZAMĀN – "Lord of the age". Title given by the **Imāmī Shī'ites** to their Twelfth **Imām** who went into occultation (**ghayba**), **Muḥammad al-Muntazar**.

ṢAḤĪFA – Lit. "leaf" of parchment or, later, of paper. – Name of the "pact" that established the **community** in **Medina** where the old **tribal** solidarity was replaced by the **solidarity** of the Muslim community. Often called the "Constitution of Medina".

ṢAḤĪḤ – "Good, valid". In legal language, adjective used generally of a tradition (**ḥadīth**) accepted as authentic. – Two collections of ḥadith, most importantly that of al-Bukhārī (died 870), bear the title *al-Ṣaḥīḥ*.

See **ḍa'if**, **ḥasan**, **mashhūr**, **mutawātir** and **qudsī**

ṢAḤN – Courtyard of a Great Mosque (**jāmi'**).

SA'Ī – "Race". One of the rituals of the **Pilgrimage** when pilgrims run between the two hillocks of **al-Ṣafa** and **al-Marwa**. – It commemorates **Ḥājar**/Hagar's journey to fetch water in the desert for her son **Ismā'īl**. – It involves several repetitions (**shawt**).

SĀ'ILŪN – "Beggars". Mentioned in the **Qur'ān** which says that they should not be rejected.

See **maskīn**, **poverty** and **piety**

SAINT, SANCTITY – Arabic **walī**, pl. ***awliyā'***, meaning "friend", whence "friend of God" and so "saint". – The idea of sanctity was not known in the early years of Islam, and not mentioned in the **Qur'ān** where reference is made only to the "pious and virtuous", the **sāliḥūn**, and those "close [to God]", the **muqarrabūn**, who number among the **elect**. – The idea was introduced through popular practices relating to "pious visits" (**ziyāra**) to the **tombs** and **mausolea** of those figures, mainly **Ṣūfīs**, who had performed "miracles" (**karamāt**), thus conferring blessings (**baraka**) that could also be gained at the **mazars** housing holy objects or spots. – This cult developed from the tenth century, while "guides to pilgrimages" began to appear in the twelfth century mentioning various "saints" including **prophets**, **Companions of Muḥammad**,

mystics (often the founders of **fraternities**), a number of jurists (**faqīhs**), various **'ulamā'** and finally some **Shī'ite imāms** and other revered **'Alids**.

SA'ĪR – The "furnace". One of the names of **Hell**, used several times in the **Qur'ān**.

See **Jahannam**, **nār** and **saqar**

SAJJĀDA – Prayer **rug**, used during ritual prayers (**ṣalāt**) for the act of prostration (**sujūd**). Usually individual and portable, they are decorated with an arched motif recalling the niche of the **mīḥrāb**. – Considered by the **Sufis** to be capable of transmitting the supernatural influence of a **saint**. Sometimes also the emblem of a **fraternity**.

See **carpet**

SAKHRA (qubbat al-) – See **Dome of the Rock**.

SAKĪNA – In the text of the **Qur'ān**, "serenity" or "presence of God who comforts Muslims in difficult times". – For **Ṣūfīs**, it has the sense of internal illumination.

SALAF – "The ancestors" or "the ancients". – Known for their **literalist** interpretations of the **Qur'ān** and chosen as guides by the **traditionalists** who see them as guarantors of fidelity to the **Sunna**.

SALAFIYYA – Movement advocating a return to the religion of the ancestors (**salaf**). – Gave rise in the nineteenth century to the tendency known as "reformism" (**iṣlāḥ**).

See **taqlīd**

SALĀM – "Salvation, peace" in a different sense from the word **ṣulḥ**. – Used several times in the **Qur'ān** where the expression *dār al-salām*, "dwelling of salvation" refers to **Paradise**. – The propitiatory value of the word is clear from its use in names for newly established towns such as ***dār al-salām* or madīnat al-salām** or in common salutations such as **al-salām 'alayka** or **'alayhi al-salām**.

See **sallama** and **salīma**

SALĀM 'ALAYKA (al-) or **'ALAYKUM** – "Peace or salvation be with you". Formula of **salutation** recommended by the

Qur'ān and properly used only between Muslims.

See **propriety**

ṢALĀT – In Iran and Turkey, **namāz**. Ritual prayer made up of formulae and actions arranged in **rak'as**. – Performed alone or in groups five times a day at specified hours calculated from the movement of the **sun** but not coinciding exactly with the main moments of this path. They are: – after dawn (**ṣubḥ**); at midday after the zenith or **ẓuhr**; in the middle of the afternoon (**'aṣr**); before sunset (**maghrib**); during the night (**'ishā'**). Performed after **ablutions**, privately on a prayer mat or in a group in a prayer hall or **masjid** such as those of a Great Mosque (**jāmi'**). – A solemn **ṣalāt** called **ṣalāt al-jum'a** is held in the Great Mosque at midday on **Fridays** when all the male members of the local **community** come together. It consists of: – an address (**khuṭba**), – an introduction in which the faithful stand with their hands raised to pronounce the formula **Allāh akbar**, "God is great", – two **rak'as**, – a formula of blessing on **Muḥammad** (**taslīm**). Other ritual prayers, sometimes optional or supplementary, are performed at particular occasions, either private or public.

See **carpet**, **nawāfil**, **tarawīḥ** and **tahajjud**

ṢALĀT al-'ĪDAYN – "Ritual prayer of the two **festivals**". Attended by large numbers of people, it can be celebrated in places other than the Great Mosque (**jāmi'**), formerly in the **muṣallā** which was outside.

See **'īd al-kabīr (al-)** and **'īd al-ṣaghīr (al-)**

ṢALĀT al-ISTISQĀ' – Ritual prayer performed outdoors "to ask for rain".

ṢALĀT al-JANĀZA – "Ritual funerary prayer". Performed after the **death** of a Muslim, either in a **mosque** or in an area close to the home of the deceased. It consists of four **rak'a**.

ṢALĀT al-KHAWF – "Ritual prayer of fear". Performed before battle when facing attack by an enemy.

ṢALĀT al-KUSŪF – "Ritual prayer of the eclipse". Held at the

Great Mosque (**jāmi'**) when there is an eclipse of the **sun** or **moon**.

ṢALĀT al-MUSĀFIR – "Ritual prayer of the traveller". Abbreviated to two **rak'a**s and performed when travelling.

ṢĀLIḤ – **Prophet** sent to the **Arab tribe** of **Thamūd**. His preaching to his people, mentioned several times in the **Qur'ān**, went unheeded.

ṢĀLIḤŪN – In the **Qur'ān**, "pious and virtuous people" on whom God bestows his blessings. Less commonly referred to as **ṣiddīqūn**.

See **maqarrabūn** and **muttaqūn**

SALIMA – "To be safe or secure". Verb giving the root for several words in the religious vocabulary.

See **aslama**, **Islām**, **Muslim**, **salām** and **sallama**

ṢALLĀ ALLĀH 'ALAYHI wa-SALLAMA – "God's blessing and salvation be upon him". – Formula that a pious Muslim should add after **Muḥammad**'s name each time it is said or written.

SALLAMA – "To give greetings of peace" (**salām**).

See **salima** and **ṣallā Allāh 'alayhi wa-sallama**

SALUTATIONS –There are many of these salutations, the use of which is required by the rules of propriety. – The formulae **al-salām 'alayka** or **'alaykum**, "Peace be with you", to which the response is **'alayka** or **'alaykum al-salām**, are properly used only between Muslims.

See **salām**

SAMĀ' – "Hearing", word with two different meanings: – a "certificate of hearing" which is the written text in which a student (**ṭālib**) declares that he has followed the lessons of a particular teacher and which certifies the content of what he learned in the course of the **majlis** ("session") of this teaching, – for **Ṣūfīs**, "musical audition" or "spiritual concerts" that play a role in the attainment of a state of **ecstasy**.

SAMAD (al-) – "The Impenetrable". One of the **Beautiful Names of God**.

SĀMARRĀ' – City in Iraq to the north of **Baghdad**, capital of the **'Abbāsid caliphs** between 836 and 892. – Burial place of two **Imāms** of the **Twelver Imāmī Shī'ites**, the Tenth, **'Ali al-Hādī**, and the Eleventh, **al-Ḥasan al-'Askarī**. – In the same **mausoleum**, known as the Mausoleum of the **'Askari-yayn**, is the spot where the Twelfth Imām, **Muḥammad al-Muntaẓar**, went into occultation (**ghayba**).

SAMĪ' (al-) – "The Listening". One of the **Beautiful Names of God**.

ṢĀMIT (al-) – "The Silent". Name used of the "hidden" **Imām** by the **Ismā'īlī Shī'ites**.

See **nāṭiq (al)**

SANJAK – Subdivision of a province in the Ottoman Empire.

See **wilāya**

SANŪSIYYA – **Ṣūfī fraternity** founded by al-Sanūsī (1787–1859) that played an important political role in the nineteenth century in North Africa and formed the basis of the State of Libya.

ṢAQĀLIBA – See **Slavs**.

SAQAR – One of the names used in the **Qur'ān** for **Hell**.

See **jahannam**, **nār** and **sa'īr**

SAQĪFA – "Covered meeting place" at **Muḥammad**'s house in **Medina**. – After his death, the **Companions** gathered here to choose his successors, the first **caliphs**, subsequently known as the **Rashīdūn**.

See **Abū Bakr** and **'Umar**

SĀRIQA – **Theft**, crime punished by a legal sentence (**ḥadd**).

SATAN – See **Iblīs** and **al-Shayṭān**.

SATANIC VERSES – Verses contrary to the idea of the **Oneness of God** that do not appear in the official text of the **Qur'ān**. Believed to have been received by **Muḥammad** from **Satan**, he then recognised that they were erroneous.

SATISFACTION (oath of) – See **Riḍwān (bay'at al-)**.

ṢAWM – Obligatory "fast", one of the pillars of Islam (**arkān al-dīn**). – Takes place in **Ramaḍān** and requires abstinence from food, drink, tobacco and sexual relations during the daytime hours from the beginning of the month to the end which can only be determined by direct observation of the **crescent** of the new **moon**.

ṢAWMA'A – Lit. "tower, retreat". Term used, particularly in the Muslim West, to refer to a **minaret**.

SAYYID, pl. **SADĀT** – "Master, lord, **noble**", whence the title **sayyidī**, "my lord", or **sīdī** in North Africa. – Often added to the title **sharīf**, especially among the **Hāshimites**, to indicate "descendants of **Muḥammad** through his daughter", the **'Alids**. – Also used on its own with the same meaning, particularly in India.

SCHISMS – See **firqa** and politico-religious **movements**.

SCHOOLS of LAW – Arabic **madhhab** pl. **madhāhib**. Sometimes known as "rites", because they deal, amongst other things, with the ritual acts required of Muslims. – They were set up in the early years of Islam, between the eighth and eleventh centuries, as jurists (**faqīhs**) formulated the method to follow in order to define the **uṣūl** ("fundamentals") of religious law (**fiqh**) and the application of them according to the "derived paths" (**furū'**). – To the four **Sunnī** schools recognised in the tenth century, after the disappearance of earlier schools such as **Ẓāhirism**, was added a **Shī'ite** school which followed the teachings of **Imām Ja'far al-Ṣādiq**.

See **Shāfi'ism**, **Ḥanafism**, **Ḥanbalism**, **Mālikism** and **rites**

SCHOOLS of THEOLOGY – See **Ash'arism**, **Hanbalism** and **kalām**.

SCIENCES – Arabic **'ilm**, pl. **'ulūm**. Theologians (**mutakallimūn**) distinguish between the "religious sciences" (**'ulūm dīniyya**) and the "secular sciences" (**'ulūm dunyāwiyya**) of which they often provide precise lists.

SEAL of the PROPHETS – Name given to **Muḥammad**.

See **khatam al-anbiyā'**

SECTS – Term used by **Sunnī** critics of deviant politico-religious

movements with a meaning equivalent to "schismatics" or "dissidents".

SELĀMLIK – Turkish name for the part of a house reserved for men.

See **harem**

SELLING or **SALE** – Arabic *bay'*. According to religious law (**fiqh**), a sale is concluded with a contract, the deed of sale (**'aqd**). Should be carried out according to precise rules that are defined by jurists (**faqīhs**) in order to guarantee equity between the two partners. As soon as the outstanding price has been paid for a sale, the purchaser receives a guarantee (**damān**) against any possible defects in the object.

See **ījāb** and **qabūl**

SERMON – Can take two different forms: – in the Great Mosque (**jāmi'**) it is the official sermon given by the **khaṭīb** with an address (**khuṭba**) that is both political and religious in content; – in a variety of other very different locations, unconnected with official meetings of the **community**, either a sermon (**wa'z**) given by a **wā'iẓ**, sometimes pietistic or **mystical** in content, or else a narrative recounted by a "popular preacher" (**qāṣṣ**).

SERVANT or **SLAVE of GOD** – See **'abd Allāh**.

SESSION – Used of teaching or spiritual concerts. See **ḥaḍra**, **majlis** and **samā'**.

SEVEN SLEEPERS (the) – See **ahl al-kahf**.

SEVENER – See **Ismā'īlis** and **Shī'ism**.

SHA'BĀN – Eighth **lunar month** in the Islamic **calendar**, often called *mukarram*, "venerated".

See **laylat al-barā'a**

SHĀDHILIYYA – **Ṣūfī fraternity** founded in North Africa in the thirteenth century by Abu'l-Ḥasan al-Shādhilī. It also spread into Egypt and south into Africa.

SHAFĀ'A – "Intercession" on behalf of sinful Muslims. – Not possible according to the **Qur'ān**. – According to the Tradition (**ḥadīth**), however, it can be exercised by **Muḥammad**

on the Day of Judgement (**yawm al-dīn**).

See **ḥawḍ**

SHĀFI‘ISM – **School of law** founded by al-Shāfi‘ī (died 820) that became established alongside **Mālikism** and **Ḥanafism** during the ninth century. It was characterised by the attempt to define very precisely the functioning of "reasoning by analogy" (**qiyās**). – It took hold mainly in the Arab East and in Iran but, during the Ottoman period, was overtaken by the increasing influence of Ḥanafism.

SHAHĀDA – "Proclamation of faith" consisting of the recitation of the formula: *Lā ilāha illā Allāh wa-Muḥammad rasūl Allāh*, "There is no god but God and **Muḥammad** is the messenger of God". – In legal language, "evidence" given in court. – More rarely, witness of the "martyr" (**shahīd**).

SHĀHID, pl. **SHUHŪD** – "Eyewitness". The presence of such a witness is mainly required when deciding on the application of a legal sentence (**ḥadd**). – An eyewitness must also legitimate all legal **deeds**.

See **‘ādil** and **qāḍī**

SHAHĪD, pl. **SHUHADĀ’** – "Witness of Islam" and "martyr". Generally one who has died on **jihād**. According to the **Qur’ān**, such a martyr will be rewarded with **Paradise**.

SHAHIDA – "To be a witness" and "to give evidence". Verb providing the root for several words in the religious vocabulary.

See **mashhad**, **shahāda**, **shāhid** and **shahīd**

SHAJARA (bay‘at al-) – "Oath of the Tree". Another name for the oath of **allegiance** also known as the bay‘at **al-Riḍwān** ("oath of satisfaction") made to **Muḥammad**. Said to have been made beneath a tree not far from **Mecca**.

SHARE – See **qirāḍ**.

SHARĪ‘A – "Law established by God". The set of rules revealed by God to **Muḥammad** that are applied to the religious and social life of the Muslim **community**. – Elaborated and clarified by jurists (**faqīhs**), specialists in religious law (**fiqh**). –

Some elements of **Sharī'a**, particularly those concerned with penal law, have been abandoned in most modern Muslim states since the nineteenth century. It is not easy to draw up a precise list of these states, nor is it clear exactly which measures merely fell into disuse and which were officially discontinued. In Saudi Arabia, however, legal sentences (**ḥadd**) are still enforced and, in a number of other countries, extremist parties see a return to the **Sharī'a** as their ideal goal.

SHARĪF, pl. **ASHRĀF** and **SHURAFĀ'** – "**Nobles**, members of the **family** of **Muḥammad**", meaning the two branches of the **Hāshimite** clan descended from Muḥammad's grandfather, Hāshim, the '**Abbāsids** and '**Alids**. – Used to refer to: local princes of **Hāshimite** origin who reigned in **Mecca** from the tenth century and were the ancestors of the ruling dynasty of present-day Jordan; or members of **Sunnī** Moroccan dynasties claiming to be descended from the '**Alids** and **Ḥasanids**, such as the Sa'dī **dynasty**, also known as **Shurafā'** and the '**Alawiyya** who still reign there today. – Prestigious title even today, either used alone or together with **sayyid**, pl. **sadāt**.

See **naqīb**

SHAṬḤ – "Ecstatic speech" attributed to a **mystic** (**Ṣūfī**).

SHAWWĀL – Tenth **lunar month** of the Islamic **calendar**, generally called **mubārak** ("blessed").

SHAWT, pl. **ASHWĀT** – One of the seven distances to and fro included in the ritual of the "race" (**sa'ī**) performed as part of the **pilgrimage**.

See **Marwa (al-)** and **Ṣafā (al-)**

SHAYKH – Or **sheikh**. Arabic term with several meanings: – man who is old and therefore worthy of respect; – master of religious **sciences** venerated for his age and his wisdom; – leader of a **Ṣūfī fraternity**.

See **pīr** and **shaykh al-Islām**

SHAYKH al-ISLĀM – Title of the highest religious authority in the Ottoman State.

See **qāḍī**, **muftī** and '**ulamā'**

SHAYṬĀN (al-) – "Satan". Name, Semitic in origin, often given to **Iblīs** in the **Qur'ān**.
See **al-rajīm**

SHEIKH – See **Shaykh**.

SHĪ'A or **SHĪ'AT 'ALĪ** – The "Party of **'Alī**".
See **Shī'ism**

SHĪ'ISM – Politico-religious **movement**, the name derived from *shī'at 'Alī* or "party of **'Alī**", formed when, after the death of **Muḥammad**, 'Alī opposed Mu'āwiya, the future **caliph** and founder of the first Islamic dynasty of the **Umayyads**, at the battle of **Ṣiffīn** in 658. – After the death of 'Alī', his supporters united first around his son **al-Ḥusayn** who was killed in 680 and then either around the descendants of the latter in two lines of Shī'ite **imāms** which separated after the time of **Ja'far al-Ṣādiq** or around the descendants of **al-Ḥasan**. In this way, a number of different branches of Shī'ism arose, including **Twelver Imāmism** which still survives in Iran, **Sevener Ismā'īlism** and **Zaydism**. – These movements and their multiple ramifications were, over the course of the centuries, the cause of many uprisings. Some failed, while others led to the formation of new states or principalities, sometimes short-lived, sometimes reliant on the national sentiment of diverse populations. – Although the total number of Shī'ites is very much smaller than that of the **Sunnīs**, the vitality of Shī'ism is still very apparent today, particularly in a country such as Iran.

SHIRK – See **associationism** and **mushrik**.

SHIRKA – In law and in commercial language, "association" between two or more people taking part together in an enterprise.

SHĪTH – Seth. Biblical figure mentioned by several authors and venerated as a **prophet** in popular devotion. – The third son of **Adam**, believed to have lived in **Mecca** and been buried near Mount Abū Qubays.

SHU'AYB – **Prophet** mentioned in the **Qur'ān**, said to have been sent to the **Arab** people of Madyan. – Identified with Moses's father-in-law and assimilated with the Biblical Jethro.

SHUKR – "Gratitude". – Gratitude to God is recommended by the **Qur'ān**.

SHŪRA – "Consultation, dialogue". Refers particularly to the meeting of eminent members of the **Quraysh** tribe after the death of **Caliph 'Umar** which led to the choosing of his successor **'Uthmān**. – It was at various times thought to be the correct way to choose later caliphs although not always supported by the theoreticians. – In modern times, Islamic states have used the principle of the shūra to justify the practice of democracy.

SHURAFĀ' – One of the plurals of **sharīf**. Used of a Moroccan **dynasty** of the sixteenth and seventeenth centuries claiming to be **Ḥasanid** and descending from **Muḥammad** through **'Alī** and **Fāṭima**. Also known as Saadians or Sa'dites.

See **Sharīf**

SHURṬA – "Police".

See **ṣāḥib al-shurṭa**

SIDDĪQŪN – **Qur'ānic** expression used of "the just". – Term subsequently widely used and applied to **saints**.

ṢIFĀT – See **divine attributes**.

ṢIFFĪN – Place in Upper Mesopotamia on the banks of the Euphrates where, in 657, the two factions within the **Companions of Muḥammad** clashed. Divided between the supporters of Mu'āwiya and the supporters of **'Alī**, their dispute was resolved by the **Judgement of Adhruḥ**. – Opposed to the decision taken at that time, the **Kharijites** left the ranks of the supporters of 'Alī.

SIGN of GOD – **Qur'ānic** expression.

See **āyāt** and **ayatollah**

SIḤR – See **magic**.

SIKKA – "Right to mint **coins**". Prerogative of **caliphs** and sovereigns.

See **coinage**

SILK – According to the Tradition (**ḥadīth**), men are forbidden to wear silk clothes.

SILSILA – "Chain of transmission". Used by **Ṣūfīs** to show the relationship of their mystic path (**ṭarīqa**) to the founder of their **fraternity**. – A novice must learn this "chain" which confers blessings (**baraka**).

See **isnād**

SIMPLICITY of ISLAM – Arabic *sadhāja*. Quality particularly extolled by Muḥammad 'Abduh, an early twentieth-century representative of reformism (**iṣlāḥ**).

SIN – Arabic *dhanab*, pl. **dhunūb** and **dhunūbāt** in a general sense found in the **Qur'ān**. – To this can be added the ill-defined idea of "major sin" (**kabīra**). The one sin that nothing can cleanse or forgive, given the special name of **ithm**, is **associationism**, the refusal to believe in the "oneness of God" (**tawḥīd**). – Other sins, mainly cultural in type, may be forgiven by God after "repentance" (**tawba**). These include a number of very serious sins, and particularly "revolt" (**ma'ṣiya**), listed in the Qur'ān and the **ḥadīth**. Various lists exist, drawn up by early writers.

See **free will**, **istighfār** and **muhlikāt**

SINCERE CULT – Expression in the **Qur'ān**.

See **ikhlāṣ**

SINF, pl. **ASNĀF** – See **trade associations**.

SIQĀYA – "Right to give water to pilgrims" in pre-Islamic **Mecca**. Granted only to a member of the **Hāshimite** clan of the **Quraysh** tribe.

See **'Abbās (al-)**

SĪRA – "Way of behaving, conduct". – Term used specifically of the biography of **Muḥammad**, *Sīrat rasūl Allāh,* written by Ibn Isḥāq and continued by Ibn Hishām (died 833) and which drew on the material found in the works called **maghāzī** ("military expeditions"). – Also used, more rarely, of biographies of sovereigns or **imāms** and of a particular literary genre of popular biographical novels.

See **ṭabaqāt**

ṢIRĀṬ – As used in the **Qur'ān**, "path", "way". – Also used of the bridge that, according to the Tradition (**ḥadīth**), the **elect** must cross to enter **Paradise** on the Day of Judgement (**yawm al-dīn**). The bridge is described as being "as fine as a hair".

ṢIRĀṬ al-MUSTAQĪM (al-) – "The right path" that all Muslims should follow. – Mentioned in the **Qur'ān**, particularly in the frequently repeated opening **sūra**, the **Fātiḥa**.

SIYĀSA SHAR'IYYA – "Policy conforming to the religious law" (**Sharī'a**). Involving the taking of measures that supplement and uphold this law, it is the prerogative of the Muslim sovereign.

See **caliph** and **sultan**

SLAVE or **SERVANT of GOD** – See **'abd Allāh**.

SLAVES – The **Qur'ān** permits slavery, recommending that the slave (**'abd**) be well treated and, if possible, eventually **freed**. **Female** slaves (**jāriyya**) may, according to religious law (**Sharī'a**), become **concubines** alongside the four permitted wives. – Slaves played an important role in Muslim society and their number, far from diminishing through the granting of freedom, increased over the course of time. This was particularly true in the case of the **slave-soldiers**, known by the general term of **mamlūk**, who played a vital role in the army. – The corps of **ghulāms** occupied an important position in the entourage of the **Abbasid caliph** and his provincial **governors**. To it were recruited both prisoners of war captured during frontier wars and mercenaries purchased from the ninth century onwards in Central Asia and Europe and later in the Caucasus. – In India, the Iberian Peninsula and Egypt, powerful **dynasties** such as that of the Slave Kings in Delhi or the **Mamlūks** in **Cairo** emerged from the ranks of these slave-soldiers.

See **devshirme**, **Slavs** and **Janissaries**

SLAVS – Arabic *ṣaqāliba*. **Slave-soldiers** from Central Europe recruited by the Muslim states of the Iberian peninsula in the Middle Ages.

SOLDIERS – See **slaves**, **Slavs**, **fatā**, **ghulām**, **Janissaries**, **jund** and **Mamlūks**.

SLAVE-SOLDIERS – Employed in the Middle Ages in a number of states in the East as guards to the sovereign. From the thirteenth century they began to be known as **Mamlūks** or, in the Muslim West, **Slavs**.

See **fatā**

SOLIDARITY – The pact of the **ṣaḥīfa**, also called the "Constitution of **Medina**", creating the Muslim **community** established the principle of solidarity, specifying that no believer (**mu'min**) can conclude peace independently of other believers. – Notion developed subsequently in relation to **piety** as defined in the **Qur'ān** which says that support should be given to less fortunate members of society, a recommendation that led to the establishment of many **charitable foundations**.

See **amāna**, **ibn al-sabīl**, **maskīn**, **sā'ilūn**, **ta'līf al-qulūb** and **yatīm**

SOUK – From Arabic *sūq*. Urban market with a characteristic organisation (small, regularly aligned shops grouped according to trade) inherited from ancient times, possibly from a Byzantine tradition, and which facilitated the task of the **muḥtasib**. – They could consist either of streets of shops and workshops or covered areas with their own architectural forms, known by various names including **khān**, **funduq** or **bedesten** which came to replace the earlier **qaysariyyas**.

SOUL – See **nafs**.

SPECULATIVE HOARDING – Economic practice condemned by Islam.

See **iḥtikār**

SPIRIT – See **rūḥ**

SPIRITUAL PATH – In **Ṣūfism** see **ṭarīqa** and **yol**.

SPIRITUAL STATES – Stages progressed through by **Ṣūfis** in the course of reaching a state of **ecstasy**.

See **ḥāl**, **manzil** and **maqāma**

SPIRITUAL UNDERSTANDING – Expression relating to mysticism.
See **ma'rifa**

STANDARDS – Arabic *'alam*, pl. *a'lām*, *raya*, pl. *rayāt*, *liwā'*, pl. *alwiya* and *alwiyāt*. Used in the army, they also appeared in Muslim cultural life as early as the time of **Muḥammad** as symbols of authority or prestige. – They accompanied the ceremonial arrival of **imāms** or other religious dignitaries, were placed around **minbars** and were fixed to the top of the **jabal al-raḥma** at **'Arafāt** at the time of the "standing" (**wuqūf**) observed by pilgrims during the **ḥajj**. – They were also used at the festivals of different **fraternities** or at celebrations at the tombs of **saints** and, in all areas, decorated a number of visited sanctuaries (**mazars**), sometimes permanently.

STATUS – See **People (status of)** and **Land (status of)**.

STRONG (the) – One of the **Beautiful Names of God**.
See **Jabbār (al-)**

SU' – See **evil**.

ṢUBḤ (ṣalāt al-) – "Dawn prayer". First of the five obligatory daily prayers. Performed before the sun starts to rise.

SUBḤA – Lit. "praise [of God]". Word used for the prayer beads used to recite the **Beautiful Names of God**.
See **tasbīḥ**

SUBḤĀN ALLĀH – "Praise to God". **Doxology** repeated frequently in the **Qur'ān** and in everyday life.

SUBMISSION to GOD – See **Islām**.

SUCCESSION – Used in connection with legal decisions.
See **inheritance**

SUCCESSOR – See **caliph**.

SUCCESSORS – Of the **Companions of Muḥammad**.
See **Tābi'ūn**

ṢŪF – "Wool". The word **Ṣūfī** is derived from the woollen garment (**khirqa**) worn by these **mystics**.

ṢŪFĪ – Representative of the **mystical** movement known as **Ṣūfism**.

ṢŪFISM – Arabic **taṣawwuf**. **Mystical** movement, the name of which is derived from the word **ṣūf**, "wool", referring to the garment of woollen patches (**khirqa**) worn by early disciples. – First recorded in the eighth century, the history of Ṣūfism has gone through a number of different phases and tendencies. In the early years, Ṣūfīs preached **asceticism** and advocated the renunciation of worldly goods, their **poverty** enabling them to arrive at true "submission" to God (**Islām**) in accordance with religious law (**Sharī'a**). Later, they stressed the struggle against human passions with the help of the heart (**qalb**), seeking **ecstasy** through union with God based on the reciprocal **love** between God and humankind mentioned in the **Qur'ān**. – Ṣūfīs or schools of Ṣūfism defined the stages (**manzila** or **maqāma**) of this mystical journey (**ṭarīqa**). At the same time, a tradition of veneration of Ṣūfī masters emerged in popular society leading to the notion of their **sanctity** and ability to confer blessings (**baraka**). – Until the ninth century, Ṣūfism was practised by single individuals in isolation, some Ṣūfīs adopting a theosophical doctrine at odds with the ideas of transcendence and the oneness of God (**tawḥīd**) and so condemned by certain **'ulamā'**. From the eleventh century, however, Ṣūfīs began to come together in **fraternities** headed by a **shaykh** where they could perform their rituals collectively, living a religious life without coming into theoretical conflict with the demands of religious law and so increasing their influence over the public at large.

ṢŪFRITES – A branch of moderate **Kharijism** that emerged particularly in western North Africa in the eighth century.

See **Azraqites**, **Ibāḍītes**, **Mzabites** and **Najadāt**

SUHRAWARDIYYA – **Ṣūfī fraternity** founded by two **shaykhs** named al-Suhrawardī who taught in **Baghdad** in the twelfth and thirteenth centuries. It flourished in Iraq and also in India.

SUJŪD – "Prostration" when the worshipper touches the ground with forehead and nose. One of the gestures used in daily prayer (**ṣalāt**).

See **masjid**, **rak'a** and **sajjāda**

SULAYMĀN – Solomon. In Turkish, Suleiman or Soliman. – Biblical figure often mentioned in the **Qur'ān** as a king, **prophet** and **rasūl** ("messenger of God") and depicted as a judge endowed with exceptional powers. Believed to have constructed the Temple in **Jerusalem**.

ṢULḤ – "Peace", in a meaning lacking the propitiatory power of the term **salām**. – Marks the end of hostilities either between Muslims or between Muslims and those non-Muslims categorised as "People of the Book" who have submitted to Islam. In the first case, it rests on a contract having generally a material object and respecting the same rules as a contract of sale (**bay'**). In the second case, it is assured by the granting of the status of **dhimma** – It is not possible to conclude such a peace with "People of the Book" who do not accept the domination of Islam. Instead, a truce (**hudna**) of limited duration, generally not more than ten years, can be drawn up.

See **dār al-ṣulḥ** and **jihād**

SULTAN – Arabic *sulṭān*, meaning "authority". – From the eleventh century, a title conferred by an '**Abbāsid** caliph on a military leader whom he invests with the necessary powers. Title taken by the various sovereigns who divided up the power in the Islamic world at that time.

SUN – Arabic *shams*. Mentioned in the **Qur'ān** as one of the **signs** of God. The movement of the sun across the sky determines the hours of the daily prayer (**ṣalāt**).

See **moon** and **ṣalāt al-kusūf**

SUNNA, SUNNĪS – The term *Sunna* ("conduct") is used to describe how **Muḥammad** acted. Recorded in the Tradition (**ḥadīth**), it became the second source of religious law (**fiqh**) after the **Qur'ān**. – Later, the followers of the Sunna and of the **community**, called Sunnīs or *ahl al-Sunna wa'l-jamā'a* found themselves in conflict with the **Shī'ites** who followed the preaching of their **'Alid imāms** whereas Sunnism was represented by the four **schools of law** that remained faithful to the tradition of the community.

SUPREME QĀḌĪ – *qādi l-qudāt* (Literally, "qadi of qadis"). Appointed as head of the magistrature at the end of the eighth century by **Caliph** Hārūn al-Rashīd. – When the **'Abbāsid** Empire collapsed, a supreme qāḍī governed in each town, controlling the activities of **qāḍīs** trained in one of a number of recognised **schools of law**, meaning that they might belong to a different school from that of the supreme qāḍī. – In the Ottoman period, this role was performed by the **Shaykh al-Islām**.

SŪRA – Chapters of the **Qur'ān** arranged according to length. Those with the largest number of verses (**āyāt**) are thought to date from the last period of **Muḥammad**'s life but, in the official version of the Qur'ān, appear at the beginning.

T

ṬĀ'A, pl. **ṬĀ'ĀT** – In legal language, concrete "acts of obedience" imposed on believers as opposed to "acts of faith" (*i'tiqādāt*). – In a general sense, "obedience", the opposite of **ma'ṣiya** ("disobedience").

TA'ĀLĀ – "May He be praised!". **Doxology** that must be used after the name of God both when speaking and when writing.

ṬABAQĀT – Lit. "classified" or "arranged" in successive layers. Whence the meaning "**biographical** dictionary", usually of **'ulamā'** or other religious figures and a number of other professional categories, where the entries are arranged in chronological order according to generation.

See **Sīra**

TĀBI'ŪN – "Followers, Successors" [of the **Companions**]. These figures come immediately after the generation of **Muḥammad**'s contemporaries who had been the eye witnesses of the events recorded by the Tradition (**ḥadīth**). –

They too are considered to be authoritative in these matters.

TABLĪGH – Lit. "transmission of a message". Now rare, this term was used to refer to the efforts to propagate Islam. – Name given to a movement founded in India c.1920 to encourage conversions. – Some extremist defenders of Islam in modern times lay claim to this term.

TABŪK – Place in Arabia, formerly close to the frontier of the Byzantine Empire, reached by **Muḥammad** in 631 on one of his military expeditions (**maghāzī**) and resulting in the submission of the inhabitants of the nearby oases. – This episode is seen as prefiguring the period of the great **conquests**.

TAFAKKUR – "Mental concentration". An exercise in spiritual training used by **Ṣūfīs**.

TAFSĪR – "Traditional **Qur'ānic exegesis** or explanation", which respects the literal meaning. – The best example is provided by the Commentary written by al-Ṭabarī (died 923).

See **Qur'ān** and **ta'wīl**

TAHAJJUD – Ritual prayer (**ṣalāt**) performed during the night.

ṬAHĀRA – "Ritual purity".

See **ablutions**

TAḤRĪF – In a theological context, "alteration, deformation". – Term used by **'ulamā'** to assert that the message of Abraham was deformed by the Jews and Christians. It is only the Muslims who have transmitted it correctly.

See **monotheism**

TAJDĪD – "Renewal" in matters of religion, based on the theories of certain **mystics** (**Ṣūfīs**).

See **mujaddid**

TAKBĪR – The action of pronouncing the **doxology Allāh akbar**.

See **kabbara**

TAKFĪR – Action of declaring that someone is an "infidel" (**kāfir**).

See **kufr**

TAKLĪF – In the language of religious law (**fiqh**), "obligation" imposed by God. – Hence the expression *taklīf mā lā yutāqu*.

See **mukallaf**

ṬALAB al-'ILM – "Study of religious science.

See **'ilm** and **ṭālib**

ṬALĀQ – "Repudiation".

See **divorce**

TALFĪQ – Lit. "assemblage". In legal language, a procedure used by modern jurists (**faqīhs**) to reconcile the various opinions of the different **schools of law** and so define a new rule.

ṬĀLIB – "Student" of religious science. – Since the eleventh century, such students have been taught at the **madāris** where they are also given board and lodging alongside their teachers thanks to the system of **charitable foundations** supported financially by the income from entailed property (**waqf**)

TA'LĪF al-QULŪB – "Gathering of hearts". Demonstrations of **solidarity** between Muslims advocated by the **Qur'ān**.

See **qalb**

TALISMAN – See **magic**.

ṬĀLŪT – Saul. Biblical figure mentioned in the **Qur'ān** as a **prophet**.

TAMATTU' – Lit. "enjoyment". In the language of religious law (**fiqh**), a way of performing the **pilgrimage** to **Mecca** where, after the completion of the **'umra** and before performing the **ḥajj**, there is a period when the pilgrim leaves the state of **holiness or purity**.

See **qirān**

TANZĪH – In the language of religion, "elimination" of the anthropomorphic elements in the concept of God. Rejection of the doctrine of **tashbīh**.

See **ta'ṭīl**

TANZĪL – Action of "bringing down", meaning to "reveal" a divine message. – Term used frequently of the origin of the **Qur'ān**, "recited" by **Muḥammad**.

See **nuzūl** and **revelation**

TAQIYA – In the language of religious law (**fiqh**), "dissimulation" practised by the followers of minority opinions within the **community**, particularly by the **Shī'ites**, in order to avoid persecution. – Practised by all Muslims with non-Muslims.

TAQLĪD – Lit. "imitation". – Refers to the attitude of those **'ulamā'**, particularly jurists and **faqīhs**, whose aim it is to imitate the ancients (**salaf**) by avoiding all innovations (**bid'a**).

See **salafiyya**

TAQWĀ – "Fear of God". Evoked several times in the **Qur'ān**. – Holds a central place in **Ṣūfīsm** since it leads to **piety** or becomes one with it.

See **muttaqūn**

TARĀWĪH – In religious law (**fiqh**), ritual prayer (**ṣalāt**) performed at night during the month of **Ramaḍān**. – Usually consists of twenty **rak'as** divided into five groups of four. The pauses at the end of each set are called *tarāwīḥ* meaning "stops", a word then extended to apply to the prayer as a whole.

ṬARĪQ – "Way", both figuratively and literally. The way of **"prophecy"** (**nubuwwa**), for example, or the path of "**sanctity**" (**walāya**).

ṬARĪQA – "Spiritual path" in **Ṣūfism**. Hence the meaning "**fraternity**".

TASARRUF – In legal language, "right of usage of property".

See **milk**

TAṢAWWUF – See **Ṣūfism**.

TASBĪḤ – Lit. "praises [to God]". Name given to the prayer beads used to enumerate the **Beautiful Names of God**.

See **subḥa**

TAṢDĪQ – In theological vocabulary, "close attachment" to the faith (**īmān**).

See **ṣiddīqūn**

TASHBĪH – "Anthropomorphism", the theological doctrine consisting of recognising in God **attributes** resembling human characteristics. – **Mu'tazilites** and **mutakāllimūn** (theologians), who adhere to a rationalising tendency in Islam, accuse **traditionalists**, the **Hanbalites** in particular, of preaching an anthropomorphism that they believe to be contrary to a belief in divine transcendence and the oneness of God (**tawḥīd**).

TASHRĪQ – Name given to the three days of the **ḥajj**, the eleventh, twelfth and thirteenth days of **dhu'l-ḥijja** when pilgrims, after a visit to **Mecca**, come to **Minā** to stone the three "piles of stones" (**jamarāt**).

TAS'ĪR – Legal term meaning the "fixed rate" or price controls enforced by the **muḥtasib**. The system is designed to prevent unreasonable price rises and hoarding (**iḥtikār**) and was used particularly in Egypt under the **Mamluks**.

See **economics** (**ethical**)

TASLĪM – "Salutations or blessings be on **Muḥammad**", the action of pronouncing the formula **ṣallā Allāh 'alayhi wa-sallama**. – Also means "submission to God" as does the word **islām** that comes from the same root.

TA'ṬĪL – Term from theological vocabulary meaning "extreme reduction of the notion of God" or the rejection of the idea of God's **attributes**. Doctrine of the **Mu'tazilites** condemned by their opponents.

See **tanzīh**

ṬAWĀF – Ritual of "circumambulation" carried out in the sanctuary at **Mecca** around the **Ka'ba**. – Pilgrims must circle a large prepared space called the **matāf** seven times, three of them running. – Takes place during the minor pilgrimage (**'umra**) or at the end of the major pilgrimage (**ḥajj**). – Also performed sometimes around the rock in the **Dome of the Rock** in **Jerusalem** or even, following popular tradition, around the **tomb** of certain **saints**.

TAWAKKUL – "Absolute confidence in God". One of the requirements of a **Ṣūfī**.

See **wakīl**

TAWALLUD – In theological vocabulary, "birth or generation of actions" in linked sequence, in other words **determinism**.

TAWBA – "Repentance". – During the **ḥajj**, Muslims express their repentance and ask God to forgive their **sins** relating to the non-observance of religious obligations (**'ibādāt**).

See **istighfār**, **kaffāra** and **God's forgiveness**

TAWḤĪD – "Oneness of God". – Fundamental belief in Islam, the rejection of which is condemned as **associationism** (**shirk**). – Nevertheless, the question of God's **attributes** has been the object of various contrary interpretations and defended by politico-religious **movements** with a wide range of viewpoints.

See **Almohads**, **sin**, **ithm**, **Muwaḥḥidūn** and **Mu'tazilism**

TA'WĪL – "Procedure of **exegesis**" of the **Qur'ān** consisting of seeking the text's "hidden meaning" (**bāṭin**). Also known as "allegorical" or "esoteric" exegesis. – Practised particularly by **Shī'ites** in order to legitimate **'Alī's** claims to power, and also used by **'Alid imāms** and **Ṣūfīs** seeking justification for their attempts to achieve a state of **ecstasy**.

See **tafsīr**

TAWRĀT – Torah, Pentateuch in the **Qur'ān**.

TAXES – See **jizya**, **kharāj**, **maks** and **zakāt**.

TAYAMMUM – Religious practice where ritual **ablutions** are performed with sand or soil in the absence of water.

See **ghusl**, **ritual purity** and **wuḍū'**

TA'ZĪR – In the language of religious law (**fiqh**), "discretionary sentence" imposed by the **muḥtasib** for crimes that are mentioned in the **Qur'ān** but do not have a fixed sanction. – Should be less severe than the lightest of the "legal sentences" (**ḥadd**) which is 50 lashes. – A regime modified during the period of the **Ottoman** Empire.

TA'ZIYA – "Poem of religious mourning", often dramatic in form and sometimes performed on a stage. In Iran and India it accompanies the **Shī'ite** festival of **'Āshūrā'** commemorating the violent death of **al-Ḥusayn**.

TEKKE – Turkish name for a **Ṣūfī** community or **monastery**.
See **khānqāh**

TENTH – Percentage of the property tax paid as a form of **zakāt** by Muslim property owners in Arabia as well as by dignitaries and soldiers benefiting from revenues from fiefs (**iqṭā'**).

TESTIMONY – Legal term.
See **shahāda**

THAMŪD – Ancient **Arab tribe** that rejected the message of the **prophet Ṣāliḥ**, an incident related in the **Qur'ān**.

THA'R – "Vengeance" in the case of **murder**. Practised in pre-Islamic Arabia under the law of retaliation (**qiṣāṣ**) and subsequently endorsed by the **Qur'ān**.

THEFT – Arabic *sāriqa*. Punished by a legal sentence (**ḥadd**) by **amputation** of the right hand if the value of the theft exceeds a certain level and has been either admitted in a confession (**iqrār**) or proven by the evidence of two eyewitnesses (**shuhūd**) (see **shāhid**). – In the case of a repeated offence, the other hand is amputated and then a foot.

THEOLOGY, THEOLOGIANS – See **kalām** and **mutakallimūn**.

THRONE of GOD – In the **Qur'ān**.
See **'arsh** and **kursī**

TIJĀNIYYA – **Ṣūfī fraternity** named after its founder in Morocco, Aḥmad al-Tijānī (died 1815). – Spread through North Africa and southwards into Africa.

TĪMĀR – Territories given on a temporary basis during the Ottoman period to military leaders required to maintain an armed body of men.
See **iqṭā'**

TIRMIDHĪ (al-) – Author of one of the six canonical collections of **ḥadīth**, he died in Tirmidh/Termez in Central Asia in 892.

TOMB – Generally **qabr** in Arabic, other terms used including **ḍarīḥ** and **rawḍa**. – The dead are buried in a tomb according to prevailing Islamic rules, generally in a cemetery lying outside a town. During the Middle Ages, however, important figures could be buried in their own house or in a **charitable**

foundation. – The Tradition (**ḥadīth**) states that tombs should not be decorated, but the custom soon arose of marking a burial place with a stele or stone cenotaph inscribed with the name of the dead person and various pious formulae. – From around the eleventh century, such funerary monuments were often contained within a **mausoleum**, some of which became highly elaborate. – At the same period some of these tombs became the object of "pious visits" (**ziyāras**), a custom that developed at the same time as the "cult of the **saints**".

See **'adhāb al-qabr** and **death**

TRADE ASSOCIATIONS – Arabic **ḥurfa**, pl. **ḥiraf**; and **ṣinf**, pl. **aṣnāf**. According to rules believed to be inherited from the Byzantine period, the different trades were grouped together in Muslim towns according to their specialisations. – The internal control of these bodies was overseen by a person in authority, the **amīn** or *'arīf*, who in early times was appointed by the market inspector (**muḥtasib**) or, around the sixteenth century in Anatolia and Iran, elected by the members themselves. – They cannot be compared with the autonomous corporations or guilds established in western Europe.

TRADITION – See **ḥadīth**.

TRADITIONALISM – Tendency characterising certain legal and theological schools consisting of the application of a traditional and **literal** interpretation of the revealed texts.

See **Ash'arites**, **ahl al-ḥadīth**, **ahl al-Sunna**, **attributes**, **Hanbalism**, **Ḥashwiyya**, **Jabrites**, **jamā'a**, **salaf**, **taqlīd**, **tashbīh**

TRADITIONIST – Not to be confused with "traditionalist".

See **muḥaddith**

TRANSMITTERS (chain of) – See **isnād** and **silsila**.

TRANSMISSION – Of important texts.

See **naql** and **riwāya**

TREE (oath of the) – See **shajāra (bay'at al-)**.

TRENCH (War or Battle of the) – See **Khandaq (Battle of the)**.

TRIBUNALS – Of the **qāḍī** or government authorities.
See **dār al-‘adl, maḥkama** and **maẓālim**

TRUCE – Between Muslims and non-Muslims.
See **hudna**

TRUST in GOD – Fundamental idea in **Ṣūfism**.
See **tawakkul**

TRUTH – In a religious and spiritual sense.
See **ḥaqq**

TURBAN – See **‘imāma**.

TWELVER IMĀMĪS – Members of a **Shī‘ite** movement that recognised **‘Alī**, his two sons **al-Ḥasan** and **al-Ḥusayn** and their descendants as the **imāms** chosen according to testamentary designation (**naṣṣ**). This line of Shī‘ite imāms came to an end with the Twelfth Imām (hence the name "Twelver"), **Muḥammad al-Muntaẓar**, "the awaited one", who went into **occultation** in **Samarra** in 874 and whose return is expected by his followers. – Imāmī Shī‘ism became the dominant religion in Iran in the sixteenth century and, in modern times, an Imāmī state was set up there in 1979. Its doctrine is, on several points, in opposition to that of **Sunnism**. The imāms of the Ḥusaynid line, who possess the impeccability and infallibility expressed by the word **‘iṣma**, are therefore the only recognised interpreters of Muslim religious law (**Sharī‘a**). Of these, the Sixth Imām **Ja‘far al-Ṣādiq** is the one whose teachings are most often quoted. – After the occultation of the Twelfth Imām, his visible representatives, called **mujtahids** and in modern times **ayatollahs**, are believed to be the sole possessors of truth and profound knowledge that without contradicting the **Qur’ān** correspond to a "hidden meaning" (**bāṭin**) that must be deciphered with the aid of symbolic **exegesis (ta’wīl)**. – In the area of law, Imāmīs have adopted a number of practices not found amongst other Muslims including temporary **marriages** (**mut‘a**), the recognition of an only daughter to be sole **heir**, the use of a modified formula for the **adhān** ("call" to prayer) and the rule of absolute obedience to the imām. – They celebrate their own festivals, most importantly the joyful celebration of **Ghadīr Khumm**, commemorating the investiture of ‘Alī by **Muḥammad** and, on the tenth day of **Muḥarram**, **‘Āshūrā’**, the ceremony of mourning marking the anniversary of the death of al-Ḥusayn at **Karbalā**.

U

UBAYY ibn KA‘B – One of the scribes to write down parts of the **Qur’ān** during **Muḥammad’s** lifetime.

See **Mu‘ādh ibn Jabal** and **Zayd ibn Thābit**

‘UBBĀD – Pl. of **‘ābid:** “ascetics” in the sense of **Ṣūfīs**.

‘UDŪL – Pl. of **‘ādil:** “official witnesses to deeds”.

UḤUD (Battle of) – Engagement in 625 between the Muslims of **Medina** and a small group of pagans from **Mecca** who had come to avenge the deaths incurred at the battle of **Badr**. – One of **Muḥammad**’s uncles, **Ḥamza**, who was renowned for his bravery, died in this battle, thus becoming a martyr (**shahīd**).

‘ULAMĀ’ – Pl. of **‘alīm**. “Scholar”, or more precisely “scholar versed in the religious **sciences**”, which are the law (**fiqh**), the Tradition (**ḥadīth**), exegesis (**tafsīr**) and theology (**kalām**). – The role of the ‘ulamā’, important from early on since they appointed themselves to give guidance to the **caliph**, became yet more central with the setting up of the **madāris** in the eleventh century. They have maintained this importance to the present day.

See **fatwā**, **ijtihād**, **muftī** and **mujtahid**

ULU’L-AMR – Expression used in the **Qur’ān** to refer to the “holders of authority”. Although Muslims owe them obedience, it is not made clear what they are called.

See **amr**, **caliph**, **Shī‘ism** and **Sunnism**

‘ULŪM al-‘AQLIYYA (al-) – The “sciences based on reasoning”.

See **'aql** and **'ulūm al-naqliyya (al-)**

'ULŪM al-DĪNIYYA (al-) – The "religious sciences" as opposed to the profane sciences or **'ulūm al-dunyāwiyya (al-)**.

See **fiqh**, **ḥadīth**, **kalām**, **madrasa**, **ṭālib** and **tafsīr**.

'ULŪM al-DUNYĀWIYYA (al-) – The "terrestrial or profane sciences" as opposed to the religious sciences or **'ulūm al-dīniyya(al-)**.

'ULŪM al-ḤIKMIYYA al-FALSAFIYYA (al-) – The "philosophical sciences".

See **falsafa** and **ḥikma**

'ULŪM al-NAQLIYYA (al-) – The "sciences based on the authority of tradition".

See **naql** and **'ulūm al-'aqliyya (al-)**

'ULŪM al-SHA'RIYYA (al-) – The "legal-religious sciences".

See **Sharī'a**

'UMAR – **Companion** of **Muḥammad** and one of the four **Rāshidūn**. As second **caliph** of Islam he reigned from 634 to 644. – His reign saw the first of the "great **conquests**" that were to lay the foundations of the future Muslim Empire. – The fiscal measures applied to the occupants of the conquered **lands** have been attributed to him.

See **kharāj** and **zakāt**

UMAYYADS – **Caliphs** of the **dynasty** founded in 660 by Mu'āwiya, **governor** of Syria and son of the **Meccan** leader Abū Sufyān whose late conversion to Islam followed **Muḥammad**'s conquest of his birthplace. They belonged to the **Quraysh** tribe but not to the **Hāshimite** clan. – After the triumph of the '**Abbāsids** in 749, an Umayyad took power in Muslim Spain, ruling in the name of an emiral dynasty whose most famous representative revived the title of caliph in the tenth century.

UMM al-MU'MINĪN – "Mother of the faithful". Name given to **'Ā'isha**, daughter of **Abū Bakr** and favourite wife of **Muḥammad**.

See **amīr al-mu'minīn** and **mu'min**

UMM al-WALAD – "Mother of a boy". **Concubine-slave** (**jāriya**) who has given birth to a son, an event preventing her master from selling her. – As a concubine of a sovereign, she would have many privileges and her son, accepted as part of the paternal family, could become heir presumptive. – In Ottoman times, when such a son came to power, his mother was given the title of "queen mother" (walide sultan).

UMMA – See **community**.

UMMĪ – Word used of **Muḥammad**, the **literal** meaning of which is "illiterate". – However, some scholars have interpreted the word as meaning "prophet of the Gentiles" since Muḥammad preached to the **Arabs** and not to the **Jews**.

'UMRA – Minor **pilgrimage** to **Mecca**. – Group of rituals that can be performed at any time of year but frequently just before or after the **ḥajj**. – It involves carrying out the ritual circumambulations (**ṭawāf**) followed by the "race" (**sa'i**). In addition, pilgrims sometimes go and drink water from the **Zamzam** well and visit various venerated places where large crowds come to make invocations.

See **ḥijr**, **maqām Ibrāhīm**, **mizāb**, **multazam** and **mustajār**

UNBELIEVER – "Infidel, miscreant, pagan".

See **kāfir**

"UNCREATED" QUR'AN – Arabic *ghayr makhlūq*. View of **mutakallimūn** (theologians) and **traditionalists** who opposed the assertions of the **Mu'tazilites** and asserted that the Word of God (**kalām Allāh**) was one of the **divine attributes** (*ṣifāt*).

UNIVERSE – See **'ālam**, **atomism**, **causality** and **creation**.

UNVEILING – Expression used in the language of mysticism.

See **mukāshafa**

'URF – "Custom, usage, **customary law**".

'URWA al-WUTHQĀ (**al-**) – Lit. "solid handle". Expression used in the **Qur'ān** to express the faith of the believer. – Title of a review (sometimes translated as "The Indissoluble Link") founded at the end of the nineteenth century by Muḥammad ʻAbduh putting forward his views on reformism (**iṣlāḥ**) and the **salafiyya** movement.

ʻUSHR – "Tenth". See **zakāt**.

UṢŪL al-FIQH – "The foundations of the law", consisting mainly of the **Qur'ān** and the Tradition (**ḥadīth**), also called **Sunna**. To these can be added, according to various principles and methods, elements that vary from one **school of law** to another. They include "consensus" (**ijmāʻ**), "reasoning by analogy" (**qiyās**) and "personal opinion" (**ra'y**). Legal treatises as such limit themselves to laying out the applications (**furūʻ**) established on the basis of these foundations.

ʻUTHMĀN – Member of the aristocracy of **Mecca** who became one of the **Companions** and the son-in-law of **Muḥammad**. One of the **Rāshidūn**, he was chosen as third **caliph** after the death of **ʻUmar**. He reigned in **Medina** from 644 to 656. – He was responsible for one of the written versions of the **Qur'ān**. – Meeting increased opposition, he was finally assassinated. This event marked the beginning of the so-called "great trial" (**fitna**) that culminated in the elimination of **ʻAlī** and the proclamation of Muʻāwiya, ʻUthman's cousin and a member of the **Quraysh** tribe (although not of the **Hāshimite** clan), the first of the **Umayyad** dynasty.

See **shūra**

V

VIZIR or **WAZĪR** – "Minister" or "assistant" of a sovereign. – Arabic term used in the **Qur'ān** of **Harūn**/Aaron, the brother of **Mūsā**/Moses. Hence its popularity in medieval Islamic times when the ʻ**Abbāsid caliphs** adopted it as title for the heads of their administration. – A word with literary resonances on account of the *Thousand and One Nights*, many of the stories of which relate to the legendary caliph Hārūn al-Rashīd and his Barmakid vizir.

VEIL – **Propriety** in Islam requires that Muslim women should only go out if their head, face and body are covered. This requirement is based on the current interpretation of a verse in the **Qur'ān** saying: "Prophet, enjoin your wives, your daughters and the wives of true believers to draw their veils close round them." – There are various names for such garments according to their different forms in different countries and periods. The word **ḥijāb** is the most general, while **burqa'** and **chador** are used further to the East.

W

WA'D wa-WA'ĪD – "Promise and threat". – Mu'tazilite principle affirming that God will carry out His threats (**'adhāb**) made to sinners without granting them remission but will fulfil His promises to the virtuous.

See **sin**, **free will**, **manzila** and **shafā'a**

WAḤDAT al-SHUHŪD – In theological language, "oneness of vision". This is the unity of the phenomenal world, as opposed to the divine world that a **Sūfī** can attain only through personal experience. Thus implies a negation of monism (**waḥdat al-wujūd**).

WAḤDAT al-WUJŪD – In theological language, "oneness of existence". This is the monism inherent in the doctrines of a **Sūfī** like Ibn al-'Arabī as well as those of the followers of many other **brotherhoods**. According to this theory, a Sūfī achieving a state of **ecstasy** believes that "All is He [God]".

WAHHĀBISM – Politico-religious **movement** derived from **Ḥanbalism**, founded by Ibn 'Abd al-Wahhāb (died 1792) who concluded a pact in 1744 with the head of the Āl Sa'ūd family of Arabia. – It laid the basis for the rigorist regime of Saudi Arabia which enforces a strict interpretation of **Sharī'a**

law and condemns certain aspects of **Sūfīsm** and also "pious visits" (**ziyāras**) to the **tombs** of the **saints**.

WAḤY – See **revelation**.

WĀ'IẒ – "Popular preacher". Also called **qāṣṣ**.

WAJD – In the language of mysticism, "love". One of the names given to **ecstasy** by the **Sūfīs**.

WAJH ALLĀH – "Face of God", in the **Qur'ānic** expression *li-wajh Allāh*, "for the face of God", meaning "for the love of God".

WĀJIB – In the language of religious law (**fiqh**), adjective used to categorise those human actions (**a'māl**) that are "obligatory or compulsory".

See **ḥalāl**, **ḥarām**, **makrūh**, **mandūb** and **mubāḥ**

WAKĪL – "Protector". – Used when speaking of God, especially in the **Qur'ānic** expression *ni'ma l-wakīl.*

See **tawakkul**

WALĀYA – "Devotion to the **imām"**, whether visible or "hidden", a fundamental obligation for **Shī'ites** who add it to the traditional pillars of Islam (**arkān al-dīn**). – In a more general sense, "saintliness", the quality of a **saint** or **walī** *Allāh*.

WĀLI – "**Governor**" of a province (**wilāya**).

WALĪ, pl. **AWLIYĀ'** – Term with several meanings including: – "friend" hence *walī Allāh,* "friend of God, **saint**", – "master, patron", giving *walī*, "matrimonial guardian", and *wali'l-'ahd*, lit. "holder of the contract", meaning "heir presumptive".

WALĪMA – "Banquet" given on the occasion of a **marriage** or a **circumcision**.

WAQF, pl. **AWQĀF** – In Turkish, *evkaf.* Called *ḥubs* or *habous* in the Muslim West. – "Property held in mortmain" declared inalienable by its owner who assigns the revenues from the property to support a **pious** or charitable **foundation**, particularly a **madrasa**, a convent (**khānqāh**), or a hospital (**māristān**).

WAQFA – "Station" on the plain of **'Arafāt** where pilgrims stand on the first day of the **ḥajj**.

See **wuqūf**

WAR, LEGAL WAR – See **battles, conquests, dār al-harb, jihād** and **maghāzī**.

WARA' – "Pious scruple". It is considered a quality of a good Muslim to have scruples.

WARNER – One of the names given to **Muḥammad**.
See **nadhīr**

WĀṢI – "Heir". **'Alī** is considered by **Shī'ites** to be the heir of **Muḥammad**.

WAṢĪYA – "Will, testament". – According to religious law (**fiqh**), it is possible to make a bequest to people other than the heirs, but only if its value does not exceed a third of the total estate. Donations are allowed as long as they involve the ownership of and profit from a property, since this arrangement makes it possible to apply the practice of mortmain (**waqf**). – In a politico-religious context, it is only among **Shī'ites** that a "testamentary designation" (**naṣṣ**) is accepted as a way of selecting a new **imām**. This usage is at variance with the Sunnī **ikhtiyār**.

WAVE – See **ifāḍa**.

WAY OF GOD – **Qur'ānic** expression.
See **sabīl**

WAZĪR – See **vizir**.

WAZN al-A'MĀL – "Weighing of deeds" of all humankind on the Day of Judgement (**yawm al-dīn**). – The **Qur'ān** says that this will be carried out by means of scales (**mīzān**). **Mutakallimūn** (theologians) have encountered difficulties in the interpretation of these verses.

WEAK – Used of a **ḥadīth**. See **ḍā'if**.

WILĀYA – In Turkish, *vilayet* or *eyalet*. "Province".

WINE – Arabic *khamr*. It is forbidden by the **Qur'ān** to drink wine.
See **nabīdh**

WIRD, pl. **AWRĀD** – "Series of invocations" recited by **Ṣūfīs**.

WISDOM – See **bayt al-ḥikma, dār al-ḥikma, ḥikma** and **ishrāq**.

WITNESS – Eyewitness. See **shāhid** and **shahida**. Witness to a deed. See **'ādil**, pl. **'udūl**. Of Islam as a martyr.
See **shahīd**

WOMEN – Arabic *nisā'*. Women are not considered equal to men in several areas of religious law (**fiqh**). – **Marriage** places a woman under the authority of her husband who may practise polygamy and unilaterally **repudiate** a wife. In law, a woman's **evidence** is worth only half of that of a man. The prescriptions in the **Qur'ān** relating to inheritance give a daughter a share only half that of a son. – The rules of **propriety** require that a woman should cover herself with a **veil** in the presence of a man who is neither her husband nor a close relative.

See **harem**

WORLD – In the sense of "universe".

See **'ālam**

WUḌŪ' –"Minor **ablutions**".

See **ghusl** and **ritual purity**

WUJŪD – "Being, existence". Philosophical term also used by **Ṣūfīs**.

See **waḥdat al-wujūd**

WUQŪF – Or *waqfa*. "Station", a ritual when pilgrims stand near **Mecca** on the plain of **'Arafat** which is dominated by the *jabal* **al-Raḥma** or Mountain of Mercy.

See **ḥajj** and **mawqif**

Y

YAHŪD – "The Jews", also called **Banū Isrā'īl** in the **Qur'ān**. Included among the "People of the Book" or **ahl al-kitāb**.

See **dhimma (pact of)**, **dhimmī**, **Khaybar**, **Medina**, **monotheism** and **taḥrīf**

YAḤYĀ ibn ZAKĀRĪYĀ' – John son of Zachariah or John the Baptist, whose birth is announced in a passage in the **Qur'ān**. – Muslim scholars have identified a number of places where his head is said to be buried. The best known is the crypt in the prayer hall of the Great Mosque (**jāmi'**) built during the **Umayyad** period in **Damascus**.

See **Zakārīyā**

YAMĪN – See **oath**.

YA'QŪB – Jacob. Biblical figure mentioned in the **Qur'ān** and referred to as a **prophet**. – Later writers describe him as the father of **Yūsuf**/Joseph and ancestor of the twelve tribes of Israel.

See **Banū Isrā'īl** and **Isrā'īl**

YASA' (al-) – Elisha. Biblical figure mentioned in the **Qur'ān**.

YATHRIB – Oasis in the Ḥijaz region inhabited in pre-Islamic times. See **Medina**.

YATĪM, pl. **YATĀMA** – "Orphan". The **Qur'ān** says that orphans should be well treated. It is forbidden to take their property.

YAWM al-DĪN – The "Day of Judgement" also called the "Day of Reckoning" or "Day of Truth". Foretold in a number of eschatological verses in the **Qur'ān**, it will follow the **resurrection** of the dead (**qiyāma**). – They will pass by the basin (**ḥawḍ**) where they will meet **Muḥammad** and then the **elect** will go to **paradise** by making the difficult crossing of a bridge (**ṣirāṭ**) from which the **damned** will fall.

See **shafā'a**

YAWM al-ḤASARA wa-l-NADAMA – "Day of Lamentation and Regret". Formula often added to "Day of Resurrection".

See **qiyāma** and **yawm al-dīn**

YAZĪDĪS – Or *Yazīdiyya*. Name derived from that of the second **Umayyad caliph** Yazīd I (died 683). – This non-**Shī'ite religious movement**, influenced by the preaching of Shaykh 'Adī (died c.1162), emerged in the twelfth century and found favour particularly among the Kurds. – Its syncretism attracted the hostility of the Ottomans in the fifteenth century.

YOL – "Way, **brotherhood**". In Turkish, **ṭarīqa**.

YŪNUS – Jonah. Biblical figure mentioned as a **prophet** in the **Qur'ān** where he is also called *Dhu'l-nūn* and, particularly, *ṣāḥib al-ḥūt*, "the man of the fish" in reference to the fish that swallowed him.

YŪSUF – Joseph. Biblical figure whose story is related in one of the **sūras** of the **Qur'ān** where he is described as a **prophet**.

– A story which partly corresponds with that in the Old Testament. – Several sites and monuments in Palestine and Egypt have connections with the story of Yūsuf.

See **Ya'qūb**

Z

ZĀHID – "Ascetic". Term used in a general way of **Ṣūfīs** who are also called "poor" (**faqīrs**) and **dervishes**.

See **asceticism** and **poverty**

ẒĀHIR – "External, exterior, literal". Adjective used to describe the obvious meaning of the **Qur'ān** as opposed to the "hidden" meaning (**bāṭin**).

ẒĀHIRISM – **School of theology and law** that emerged in Iraq in the ninth century and which became influential particularly in Muslim Spain in the eleventh century. – The name derives from the fact that its followers observed a rigorously **literal** (**ẓāhir**) interpretation of the **Qur'ān** and the **ḥadīth**.

See **traditionalism**

ZAKĀRĪYĀ' – or Zachariah. Biblical figure mentioned in the **Qur'ān** as a **prophet** and the father of **Yaḥyā**/ John the Baptist. – His **tomb** is believed to be in **Jerusalem** in the cave in the **Dome of the Rock**.

ZAKĀT – "Obligatory **alms**". Tax, the payment of which is one of the "pillars of Islam" (**arkān al-dīn**) and which purifies Muslims from the stain of sin. – In early times, zakāt was levied on livestock, corn, fruit, gold and silver and merchandise. Later, such goods were subject to other taxes but the **tenth** (*'ushr*) applied to the harvest of certain lands belonging to Muslims continued to be known as zakāt.

ZAMZAM – Well near the **Ka'ba** in **Mecca** where a ritual dating from the Middle Ages states that **ḥajj** and **'umra** pilgrims must drink the water and sprinkle it on their garments. – The spring is believed to have been that from which **Ismā'īl** and his mother **Ḥājar**/Hagar drank.

ZANDAQA – Word of Persian origin meaning the "impiety" or "**heresy**" of which an eighth-century group known as *zindīq*, pl. *zanādiqa* were accused. They were converts who had secretly remained faithful to their earlier Manichean religion and who were sometimes condemned for **apostasy** (**ridda**).

ZĀWIYA – In Turkish, *zaviye*; in North Africa *zaouia*. **Ṣūfī monastery** or community. – Such buildings, around which important sanctuaries developed, are particularly widespread in North Africa.

ZAYD ibn 'ALĪ ibn al-ḤUSAYN – An **'Alid** and grandson of **al-Ḥusayn**, he rebelled against the **Umayyad caliphs** and was killed in 740. – The **Shī'ite** movement known as **Zaydism** takes its name from him.

ZAYD ibn THĀBIT – One of the scribes who wrote down parts of the **Qur'ān** during the lifetime of **Muḥammad**.

See **Mu'ādh ibn Jabal** and **'Ubayy ibn Ka'b**

ZAYDISM – Politico-religious **movement** of **Shī'ite** origin deriving its name from **Zayd**, grandson of **al-Ḥusayn**. – Its followers recognised as an **imam** any **'Alid** descended from al-Ḥusayn or **al-Ḥasan** who had resorted to violence to take power. Unlike most other Shī'ite movements, they did not endow their imams with any supernatural qualities nor did they select them by "testamentary designation" (**naṣṣ**). – Zaydism gave rise to a number of short-lived revolts but also established two **dynasties**, one in Ṭabaristān that lasted from the ninth to the eleventh century, the other in the Yemen, also established in the ninth century but remaining in power until 1962.

ZAYN al-'ĀBIDĪN – "Ornament of the faithful". Title given to **'Alī al-Aṣghar**, son of **al-Ḥusayn**, Fourth **Imām** of the **Imāmis** and Third Imām of the **Ismā'īlis**.

ZĪJ, pl. **AZYĀJ** – **Astronomical** table that, amongst other things, enabled scholars to determine the correct orientation of the **qibla**.

ZINĀ' – "Fornication or adultery". For a man this means having illegal sexual relations with a **woman** who is neither his wife nor his slave-**concubine**. For a woman, it means having sexual relations with a man who is neither her husband nor her master. – According to the Tradition (**ḥadīth**), the punishment is death by stoning (**lapidation**). The **Qur'ān**, on the other hand, states that the punishment should be 100 lashes and then only if formal evidence (**shahāda**) is provided by four male witnesses. This "legal sentence" (**ḥadd**) was abolished along with others in the Ottoman Empire in 1858. It continues only in those States where the religious Law (**Sharī'a**) is strictly enforced where it is used particularly in cases of women accused of adultery.

ZINDĪQ – Guilty of a particular form of **heresy**, **zandaqa**.

ZIYĀRA – "Pious visit" to a venerated site (**mazār**). – The veneration of holy places such as a **tomb**, **maqām** or **mashhad** of a **saint**, **prophet** or **shahīd** is popularly believed to confer blessings (**baraka**) on the believer. – The practice of such visits became widespread from the twelfth century although condemned by certain rigorist **fuqahā'** (sing. **faqīh**) and more particularly by the followers of **Wahhābism**.

ZOROASTRIAN – See **mājūs**.

ZUHD – See **asceticism**.

ẒUHR (**ṣalāt al-**) – "Midday prayer". Second of the five obligatory daily prayers (**ṣalāt**). It takes place just after the **sun** has passed its zenith.